125 Wow! Change

Tools For Leaders During Change

Christina M. Battell

and

Deborah C. Miller

DISCLAIMER / LEGAL NOTICE

Table of Contents

INTRODUCTION

Chris Battell and Deb Miller are friends and colleagues who share a love for adventure. Learning provides one of their favorite types of adventure. So, Chris—who works with leaders, teams, conflict, meetings and the like—and Deb—whose specialties are projects, efficiency, technical writing, and process improvement (amongst other things)—took on the adventure of studying change literature. They had noticed that their own success depends on their respective abilities to change a variety of things, including themselves. They also saw that their clients needed the same ability to change.

With a destination clearly in mind—discover the best and proven ways to change and change for good—the two embarked on the journey. They traveled through the contents of many a book on change. The two of them visited with respective clients about change. They made observations about change and its role in their personal and professional lives. They talked with colleagues, read blogs and participated in conversations about change on LinkedIn.

Chris and Deb also tried things. They used change principles and practices with clients. And, like Mad Scientists mixing weird concoctions and cures, even tried out a few of their newly discovered potions for prying loose of the status quo—on themselves.

They experimented—admittedly with some failures. After each set-back, the two picked themselves up, continued the research, reading, and discussions and continued on their way. Sometimes, there were side trips to locations just off the beaten path of change, but still quite related to it—mini-adventures inside the bigger adventure. And, there were many successes which seemed very much like the moments of a trip when one arrives at an astonishing site or discovery, steps back in awe, delight, clarity or some equally compelling emotion, and takes a picture to catalogue the precious experience for posterity.

And what is catalogued ought to be compiled. This book is one result of the compilation of the journey's most enlightening moments. We hope you find it useful and enjoyable.

THE CHALLENGE OF CHANGE

More than one expert has said that the only constant in life is change. The statement—stated so often that it's become cliché—is true nonetheless. Even those who don't want to change—and there are plenty—find themselves forced out of complacency, like it or not. Here's why.

There are external pressures.

- Local competition
- Global competition
- Financial pressures
- Technological advances
- Customer and shareholder expectations
- Political and economic uncertainty
- Government regulation
- And on, and on, and on…

There are internal pressures.

- Top Management and Board expectations
- Management expectations all around, at all levels
- Competing political agendas

- Employees, from disgruntled to fearful to sabotaging

- Silos in conflict

- Strategic goals

- Short-term goals

- Mounting deadlines and demands

With stressors like these, it's inevitable. Companies that want to survive must change. And companies who want to do more than survive—those who want to thrive—must change even more. Somehow. Some way. Wise leaders know it's so.

Change Efforts Can Fail

Yet ironically, management gurus who study and measure such things tell us that most formal organizational change efforts fail, in at least one significant aspect. Some say the failure rate is as high as 85%. In the real world it looks like this. A company gets in a game of change with the highest aspirations and most promising vision only to throw in the towel after just one inning. Score? Progress 0. Cynicism 5.

It's no wonder that so many employees complain about the "flavor of the month" initiatives in their companies. Given the dismal statistics about the success of change, they're right. Consider just two of the most common types of initiatives that fall into the change category—process improvement and technological advances. How often do those initiatives fail to produce desired results? Estimates range from 60-70% of the time. Not so good.

But there IS something good. When a company DOES achieve successful change, the results typically stand out. They're startling. And profitable. Consider Jack Welch, former CEO of GE. He led GE through successful organizational culture shift, now heralded in many articles and books. What's all the fuss about? Well, in the case of GE, some powerful and compelling words come to mind. Innovation. Agility. Performance. Extraordinary leadership. Over the span of Welch's tenure at GE, his efforts at leading change ultimately resulted in profits. Big profits.

Looking at the astonishing results at GE (and others like the IBM turnaround and the Virginia Mason transformation, to name just two), it's no surprise that other top management teams have wanted and still want to get into the change game. So, how to set the stage for extraordinary change? How to navigate the churning waters of the change journey? How to keep from throwing in the towel before the big win? In short, how to transform change into real competitive advantage?

Change experts offer lots of answers to those questions. And WOW! Change Cards dispenses those answers and other expert advice in small, easy-to-digest bites. We cannot take credit for the ideas. We can take credit for packaging them in a way that is easy to sort, digest, and do.

Change Is Just A Card Away

Well, more realistically, change is many WOW! Change Cards away. But WOW! Change Cards are an easy-to-use tool to support you through change. WOW! Change Cards will give you a change education. Offer solid change advice. Lift sagging change spirits. Stimulate some robust change conversations.

WOW! Change Cards can be used by:

- Individuals
- Facilitators
- Trainers
- Executives
- Business owners
- Managers
- Supervisors
- Departments
- Teams
- Leaders of all kinds

In so many ways:

- Self-directed learning
- Self-reflection
- Classroom training
- Staff meetings
- Retreats
- Department bulletin boards
- Brainstorming sessions
- Planning meetings

- Team building sessions

- Project management

- Progress meetings

- Settings of many types

In order to:

- Study change concepts, techniques, and ideas—at your own pace, one small bite at a time.

- Equip executives, managers, supervisors and employees at all levels with change advice, on the spot.

- Stimulate group discussion about important change questions and issues.

- Infuse spirit and fun into even the most serious business discussions.

- Reinforce classroom training change lessons.

- Get everyone—not just a dominant few—involved in change discussions.

- Help people think "outside the box."

- Support people through the stress of change.

- Fulfill the adult learning needs for auditory, visual, and kinesthetic learning methods.

- Keep meetings, training, and other sessions lively and fast paced while focusing on the topic of change.

- Take change lessons and inspiration "to go." Review them anytime and anyplace.

- Display one change lesson per day. On your desk, or a table, or a mirror. Anywhere.

- Manage the stress of change in your life and work.

LEADING: FACE CHALLENGES

The Ten Challenges Of Change

The Human Response

From start-up to hardwiring to redesign—there are some predictable responses to change. In ***The Dance of Change***, Peter Senge and crew organized those responses into Ten Challenges of Change. Understand the challenges—and how to deal with each—and be better prepared to lead change effectively. Read each challenge (some take up more than one card) and assess whether that challenge is one your organization needs to be well prepared to tackle. Then, get the right people involved with the challenge and tackle it head on.

YOUR NOTES:

1 Challenge Of Change: Not Enough Time

How to Create Time Flexibility

Good intentions, high motivation, and a solid business case are not enough. Successful change requires a lot of time. Time for new meetings. Time for training, collaborating, conversing, and planning. Emails about the change take time. Reading about the change takes time. And the list of time eaters goes on. The issue of where to find enough time is what the Challenge of Change "Not Enough Time" addresses.

For change to be successful, management must realize that it cannot just pile the activities of change on top of existing work. Some old activities must go to make room for the new. This is why Senge has spoken of the Challenge as one of "not enough time flexibility" as opposed to literally "not enough time."

What to do? Senge suggests several things:

- Schedule time to focus and concentrate on change activities. Focusing and concentrating contribute to change success far better and sooner than just "fitting change in".

- Quit playing political games that just slow things down. Guard time fiercely by dealing with what's important and communicating directly. Spend time with people and in meetings where the agenda is substantial and relevant, not just for show.

- Say "no" to every non-essential activity. If an activity is not aligned with the most important goals and actions plans of change, consider putting it on the Not To Do list.

When can you schedule time for change in your schedule?

What non-essential activity can you say "no" or put on your Not To Do list?

2 Challenge Of Change: Not Enough Time

The GE Work-Out—One tool used for the GE transformation.

Jack Welch called one of the tools of transformation at GE Work-Out for good reason. Work-Out was meant to stand for, taking excess "work out" of the system. Excesses such as those that existed at GE during Welch's tenure, exist in every organization to some degree, caused by outdated methods and other types of bureaucracy. The idea behind Work-Out was a simple one: to free people's time for the really important activities and at the same time, refuse falling into the trap of accomplishing only the urgent or the status quo. Work-Out was/ is a powerful tool for translating organizational imperatives into individual action. Work-Out provided guidance for employees' daily decisions and actions.

In the beginning, Work-Outs included GE people from across functions and levels. Those cross-functional and multi-level Work-Out teams examined work practices, using a tool called RAMMP:

R = **Reports:** Is this report really necessary?

A = **Approvals:** Does the decision need so many approvals?

M = **Meetings:** Do we need to have this meeting?

M = **Measures:** Are we measuring what is important?

P = Policies and Procedures: Are policies and procedures helping or hindering work?

In addition to squeezing out the excess of non-essential action, Work-Outs fulfilled another critical benefit. Work-Out taught people to apply critical thinking to their daily activities, encouraging them to frequently ask the strategic question, "Why are we doing this?" The lesson to the examination was and is, if an activity is not worthy, do not do it.

What are the RAMMP items in your area?

3 Challenge Of Change: No Help

Coaching Change Success

It happens all too easily. Top management spends many meetings discussing the need for change. They build the business case, amassing, analyzing and discussing lots of data to arrive at the benefits and obstacles to change. They become convinced of the necessity of the change for the organization. They communicate what they believe to be the essentials of the case for change to their direct reports. And, they expect the word to move down the chain in order for the change to unfold. The problem is, somewhere, somehow the message gets stalled along the way. And those at the front lines—like many others in the organization—end up feeling like they're operating in the dark instead of the light during change. No Help is a Challenge of Change that surfaces when people in organizations of all kinds and in all types of changes express frustration over not knowing what to do. Sure, the overall knowledge that change is happening is often pretty well known. But, equally often, the details about what to do during change remain murky at best.

Where's the guidance? What are the right steps to take? Who can tell us what to do next? What are the real priorities? How will we know that we've succeeded? Those are the questions and unfortunately, they often remain unanswered or poorly answered.

To navigate change successfully, wise leaders seek guidance and counsel, whether from inside or outside of the organization.

Where is the best place to get help for the No Help Challenge? An excellent coach.

Some organizations create a pool of internal coaches to support people through change. Some hire outside coaches to do the same. Others rely on traditional managers to fulfill the change coaching role. No matter what path—or combination of paths—your organization takes, discover who your best change coach will be. Then, seek that coach's help.

> *Who do you rely upon for guidance*
> *during change?*

4 Challenge Of Change: No Help

The Change Coach—*Don't go it alone.*

Great change coaches are like great coaches in general. They:

- Possess mastery in their area of coaching expertise.
- Can share favorable testimonials from other clients.
- Ask fabulous, probing, stimulating, enlightening questions.
- Listen, listen, listen so that clients feel truly heard, valued and understood.
- Know how to balance questioning and listening with giving feedback and directing.
- Hold clients (employees) accountable.
- Help clients examine "blind spots"—areas of strength or weakness that the client is currently unaware of.

Great coaches do all of this and much more. Top performers seek coaching in order to become better than ever. You should do the same.

> *Who is coaching you through change?*

5 Challenge Of Change: Not Relevant

Deepening the Commitment to Change

People in organizations are stretched, overloaded, and in general, doing more with less these days. Accepting one more assignment, no matter how important or inviting, is not easy. To tackle change effectively, the case in favor of the change must be convincing enough for people to take on one more thing—maybe more—and do it well.

To buy into the case for change, people must be clear about and convinced of two things:

1. How will the change fulfill key business needs, significantly benefitting the company?

2. How will the change affect me, what can I contribute, and what's in it for me to do so?

Answers to #1 outline the business case for change. Answers to #2 address the people side of change. Both questions—properly and thoroughly answered—provide information to deepen commitment and strengthen buy-in on the part of stakeholders of all kinds, but particularly employees who must execute plan details.

Why are we undertaking this change?

YOUR NOTES:

6 Challenge Of Change: Not Relevant

Focusing On The Transformation—Some key questions to consider…and answer.

The Case For Change: Important Questions

Gather the change leaders together and answer these questions, thoroughly, completely, and specifically. Organize groups of other people within the organization to discuss the questions with answers as well. To change effectively requires plenty of thoughtful discussion, so use these questions to fulfill that requirement.

1. Why is the change urgent?

2. What will happen if we don't undertake this change?

3. What results do we want to produce?

4. What are the steps to achieve this change?

5. Who will be involved in each step?

6. Who are our greatest supporters and detractors of the change?

7. What specific actions must each role within the organization take to support the change?

Experts agree that creating a case for change that arouses a sense of urgency in people sets a strong tone for change success.

Assuming that is the case, spend plenty of time on all of the questions, but especially questions #1 and #2.

What is your case for change?

7 Challenge Of Change: Walking The Talk

Be an Impeccable Role Model for Change

In the midst of change—when the troops are feeling the heat—they'll likely ask themselves if their leaders are walking the talk of change. If you're a leader, that means employees will be scrutinizing you. Words alone won't convince others of your commitment to change, but actions that endorse those words will turn the tide.

The trouble is, we humans have a knack for self-deception and that includes the leaders among us. We can be quite blind to some of our weaknesses or hypocrisies. It's the human condition. Knowing this, wise leaders assume they will not "Walk the Talk" perfectly. They purposely seek feedback to shine a light on blind spots in order to correct them. They ask a trusted few to point out where their words and actions do not match. In other words, they make sure that "the emperor is wearing clothes". The questions are:

1. How well am I walking the talk?

2. Do I spend my time in ways that align with and support the change or contradict it?

3. Are my decisions properly aligned with the critical elements of the change?

4. Do I spend meeting time with items critical to the change or is the time spent with business as usual topics only?

> *How well are you "walking the talk?"*
> *How do you know?*

8 Challenge Of Change: Walking The Talk

Present The Case For Change

Here's an acronym for crafting a KWIC change message…or any other message, for that matter.

The next time you need to create and present the case for a change (or anything else), apply the KWIC formula. Credit for the formula goes to Marlene Caroselli.

K = Kernal; the essence of your remarks; the main point.

"We face challenges this year like we never have before. This change will prepare us to battle those challenges. Let me share more about what I mean."

W = Widen; expansion of the main point; more information to explain the main point.

"As you know, our main competitor, Joe Corp, has introduced a new kind of software that our clients have yearned for. They beat us to the punch. Now we must catch up. No, now we must pass them in the race."

I = Illustrate; examples or details to clarify the message.

"Joe Corp has captured 24% of market share that was once ours. Add to that, our clients say they are elated to have the capabilities that Joe Corp's new software offers."

C = Conclude; summarize the message and give a call to action.

"So, the competitor has caught us sleeping at the switch, has managed to listen to clients better than we have, and has come up with a superb innovation. We can undoubtedly catch them. We can pass them. But we need the best of the fine talent in this company. That's all of you. I ask you to help."

What message can you use KWIC to create?

9 Challenge Of Change: Walking The Talk

Experts Say to 'Over-communicate' during Change, But How?

Keep the 3 'A's in mind as you communicate through change.

Clear communication is structured communication. For example, convincing communication appeals to emotions. Compelling communication includes audience involvement. Use the 3 'A's formula to help make critical change messages clear, convincing and compelling.

A = APPEAL

To peoples' emotions, not just to their logical minds; to a sense of justice and fairness; to a larger cause, adding meaning; to the message receivers' WIIFM (What's In It For Me?).

A = ANTICIPATE

The potential questions, objections and reactions of the audience.

A = ASK

For their commitment and help to succeed; provide a call to action.

> *How can you apply the 3 'A's to a change message?*

YOUR NOTES:

10 Challenge Of Change: Walking The Talk

Ben Franklin's Thinking Tool: Pros and Cons

The famous founding father is well known for many things, one of which was his practice of making decisions by listing Pros and Cons. Help beef up planning and help others think things through by using Benjamin Franklin's technique of deliberately analyzing Pros and Cons. Individually or with a group, list the following and discuss.

P = PRO

What are the advantages of this decision/course of action/idea?

C = CON

What are the disadvantages of this decision/course of action/idea?

D = DISCUSS

What needs further discussion?

Think of a situation,
decision,
course of action,
or idea where you can use PCD?

YOUR NOTES:

11 Challenge Of Change: Walking The Talk

Both Sides Now: A Creative Viewing, Critical Thinking Skills Activity

The Chinese philosopher, Lao-Tzu said "…learn to see things backward, inside out, and upside down."

"Why bother?" you might ask. It's so much quicker and easier to simply look from one perspective. But, your convenience—or mine, or anyone else's—is not the point. Many great things have been discovered by taking the backwards, inside out and upside down perspectives. For example,

Upward evaluation: Employees evaluating their managers.

Viral marketing: Giving things away to make money.

Listen to criticism: Asking for more criticism instead of defending one's position.

How to use this concept of creative viewing? List some problems that your group faces. Ask the group to pick a problem and view it from backwards, inside out, and upside down. Expanding on the concept, some other questions to stimulate creative thinking follow. Begin each with the starter, "What if we took the problem and…"

- Did the opposite?
- Made it bigger?

- Made it smaller?

- Added to it?

- Subtracted from it?

- Did it in reverse order?

- And so on...

> **To what problem can you apply creative viewing?**

12 Challenge Of Change: Walking The Talk

A Change Discussion Technique: Ask for what's wrong with the change...on purpose.

Devil's Advocate

Take charge of change objections by actively soliciting them and not just waiting for objections to come up. To do so, put the following question on your agenda regularly. Don't just include the question at the beginning of change, but at intervals throughout the change.

What Is Wrong With This Change?

Ask that people be candid—respectfully open and honest. Also ask that all ideas be accepted. List the answers on a board or flipchart. The process could be called ***Objections Brainstorming***. Once the list is finished, pick the top 3 objections and answer those. Another option for answering objections: assign several people to research a top objection more thoroughly and report back findings to the whole group.

What to include in order to effectively answer objections? Facts, figures and date are a good start as they complete the real story of change and help clear up misunderstandings. Possible solutions for resolving an objection point to a positive future that people can anticipate. Adding the potential upside of any objection—the potential benefit—balances the downside that people so easily focus on. If you want to personally address objections, fine. But, putting others in charge of the work of answering objections educates them and deepens commitment to the change.

> ***What are some objections people
> have regarding the change?***
>
> ***How can we overcome the objections?***

13 Challenge Of Change: Walking The Talk

Understand How They See It

Use the power of metaphors to gather views of the change.

Aristotle said, "To understand the metaphor is the beginning of genius." Use the power of metaphor to get people's views about change. Define the term metaphor: "a comparison between two things not usually compared" and explain the purpose of metaphor: to make an abstract concept clear by comparing it to something concrete, well known, and understood. Give some examples.

- Women's inability to be promoted to the highest levels in the workplace: glass ceiling

- Communism's power to separate: the iron curtain

- Communism: the evil empire

- Cold feet; broken heart

- Flagship enterprise

- Margaret Thatcher was the iron fist in a velvet glove

- Life is a bowl full of cherries

- Life is like a box of chocolates

- Life is a yo-yo with lots of ups and downs

Ask participants of a group or team to imagine a metaphor to best represent their feelings about the current change. Give them time to write the metaphor. Ask volunteers to share.

What will you learn from the exercise? You will hear peoples' candid views about the change. You will be introduced to the humorous side of the organization's change. You will broaden your own perspective of change with interesting and perhaps provocative ways the change is seen by others. You may even discover elements of the change to improve.

> ### *What metaphor best represents the current change?*

14 Challenge Of Change: Fear And Anxiety

The Price of Progress: Uncertainty

Ironically, although fear and anxiety are considered challenges of change, they are also signs of the progress of it. Since fear and anxiety are an inevitable part of transition from the old to the new, it's healthier to recognize and accept the emotions than it is to battle them. Add to that, when fear and anxiety crop up, they can be viewed as progress through the cycle of change and not just a barrier to it.

As change evolves, fear and anxiety are replaced by acceptance of a new reality. Acceptance is reached at different times with different people, in part depending on how quickly those same people gain confidence in their abilities to handle the change competently, correctly and professionally.

Take the current day push for transparency, as one example. The old way of handling mistakes in many organizations was to sweep the mistakes under the rug, cover up what went wrong, and pretend that all was well. The new way is to talk openly about mistakes, discussing how they happened, how to recover and learn from them, and how to install preventive measure and solutions. The first few times a person accustomed to the old way is faced with open discussion of mistakes via the new way, one can imagine the anxiety. As the same person experiences a boost of confidence from facing mistakes, one can just as easily imagine the anxiety and fear.

Smart leaders put themselves in others' shoes, imagine their fears during change, and help them through the uncertainty of transition. Possessing empathy as well as business sense, they have a plan for managing the people side of change. They learn how to communicate at a heart level as well as they communicate at a head level. They ask good questions and they listen beyond words to what is really being said.

How are people demonstrating fear and anxiety in your organization?

15 Challenge Of Change:
Fear And Anxiety

More On Fear And Anxiety: What Arouses Fear and Anxiety.

To better understand the fear and anxiety that full-fledge adults suffer through change, consider the following questions weigh on their minds.

Am I safe? Or am I vulnerable?

People wear a variety of masks in life and at work. The purpose of these masks is to create a sense of security and safety by living up to habitual, imagined expectations. For example, there's the person who always shows a polite face, refusing to create waves in smooth waters. There are those who please people at all costs, even when that cost is their own desires. There are those who seek continual perfection, protecting themselves against the risk of even the smallest human error. And there are those who seek safety by criticizing others before they can be criticized.

When we ask people to change, the shift threatens the cover of many of those roles. People feel exposed by having to face the prospects of speaking up, asking for help, making mistakes, taking initiative, losing efficiency, giving up power and the like. What fears do you and others experience during change?

Am I adequate? Do I measure up?

Most employees treasure their ability to get things done. They value their knowledge, skills and competence. They like to consider themselves good, solid performers at the very least. They may see themselves as top performers at the very most. Change demands that people try new methods, acquire new knowledge and learn new skills.

People may wonder if they're up to the challenge as they imagine slogging through rather than breezing through new skills. Can you blame them? Are you up to learning new knowledge, skills and methods posed by change?

Can I trust myself? Can I trust others?

What if your department or organization conducted themselves disrespectfully once upon a time? Perhaps people were victims of intimidation, exploitation or broken promises? If the answer is yes, then your organization is not alone as such conduct became the norm in too many organizations.

If it's not bad enough that such conduct happens at all—as strange as it seems—people actually get used to behavior they are regularly subject to. Perpetrators and victims alike get used to it. Bad behavior becomes "normal."

When change asks that disrespectful conduct becomes respectful, the hurdles are many, but one of the biggest is the sheer discomfort of adjusting to more positive behavior and giving up the comfort of the negative.

When yesterday's management style won't work for tomorrow's organization, face the fact that the change is hard.

> *Are leaders and employees prepared to behave in accordance with the needs of change?*

YOUR NOTES:

16 Challenge Of Change:
Fear And Anxiety

Facing Fear And Anxiety

Do YOU need to work through some fear and anxiety? Here's an activity for you.

Reflect On This

1. **How do I know when I am fearful or anxious?** What are the physical, mental, emotional and behavioral symptoms? Shaking? Racing thoughts? Upset stomach? Raised voice? Procrastination? Distraction? Fast, shallow breathing?

2. **When I become defensive, what triggers it?** Angry expression? Disagreement? Raised voices? Mistakes? Someone saying no? Trying new things? Vague answers to questions? Unclear expectations?

3. **What do I believe that creates the fear and anxiety?** Situations don't create our feelings. Our thoughts—which we control—about those situations creates our feelings. Do you think that making mistakes makes you a bad person? Do you believe that professionals never lose emotional control and always have perfect command over their emotions? Do you believe that you should fulfill every expectation asked of you? Your thoughts create your feelings, so it pays to know what thoughts create fear and anxiety. Then change those thoughts. Talk to yourself as

you would talk to a best friend. Change your mind, change your feelings.

4. **How could others help me?** What kind of help can you seek to more positively cope with the fear and anxiety? For example, can you ask a colleague to be a sounding board for feelings? Or, can you check ask what boss really thinks about mistakes? Can you engage in dialogue about new expectations for your position? Would it be wise to get coaching for new skills?

> *What have you learned from this self-reflection activity?*

17 Challenge Of Change: Assessment

Many leaders believe that "the results will speak for themselves." A new product's success will be obvious. The advantages of a new method will be widely and easily recognized, embraced and adopted. The wondrous results of change will glare at people like neon lights. Right? Don't bet on it!

One reason people don't quickly and easily see the positive impact of change is they don't know what success should look like. In other words, they don't know how to evaluate progress or results of change. Traditional and therefore, well known and understood measures, may not shine a proper light on a new product, service, or method's success or failure. Sometimes and ironically, even when a change is VERY successful, traditional measures may make it look bad.

Take process improvement for example. The savings of a process improvement initiative may not show up on the balance sheet, even as the investments of the same process improvement— people and time—may be quite obvious on the balance sheet. On the face of it, some changes can appear counter-productive even when they're not.

How easily will people see the
success of change?

YOUR NOTES:

18 Challenge Of Change: Assessment

A Measurement Story

If you want successful change, measure the right things. Quantity and customer satisfaction may have to duke it out for top priority. Which measure better demonstrates change success?

There once was a company where everyone evaluated success by how many pieces were produced. Every day, every week, and every month employees knew not only how many pieces were being produced but each employee could compare individual productivity with the whole. The numbers were posted and productivity equated with success.

However, the company executives also knew they had a reject problem, resulting in a customer satisfaction problem and an efficiency problem. So, they told the people:

"You need to work better as a team. You need to cut down on rejects. Improve your methods. But still be very efficient. We must satisfy customers and all these things will help with that."

The leaders announced the change repeated the message to the workers many times. Still, not much changed. Why? If you talked to any worker, the answer would be clear:

"We get paid by how much we get done. If we worry about rejects, or rework, or teamwork, or customers, it just slows us down. We will not be successful and worst of all, we will not get our bonus."

People knew they were successful by how success was measured and by how they were paid for that success. The strategies for change, that the executives insisted were so important, were not measured at all. And, even if they were, the employees understood on which strategy for success their bread was buttered. Why change?

> *How do you measure the success of the change?*
>
> *How do the old ways of measuring success interfere with new measurements?*

19 Challenge Of Change: Assessment

Another Measurement Story

What gets measured gets done.

From The World Of Sales

A sales team learned a new way to sell. The new way focused on building solid relationships with clients, large and small. The approach was more "consultative," meaning that sales people sought to create true partnerships with clients. They conversed, questioned, and listened more. They spent time discussing things deeply enough to discover more innovative solutions to fulfill clients' needs. All of this discussion led to a lot more time talking with clients.

The time showed up as increased "cost of sales" and decreased number of sales calls figures. Oops! The sales people soon lost interest in the new selling method.

> *What are the "cost of sales" figures*
> *related to your change?*
>
> *How do they slow down change progress?*

YOUR NOTES:

20 Challenge Of Change: Assessment

Another Measurement Story

How you're measured influences how others view you.

Perceptions Count

A team of engineers in charge of product innovations decided to become more transparent, including more open and honest communication. Instead of hiding problems, they decided to share problems openly within the team. Why? They knew they could solve problems faster and better that way. And they were right.

Their new way of doing things—sharing problems openly to resolve them—did save a lot of time and money, which the engineers found encouraging. Conversely, the visibility also exposed what were considered, "engineering change orders." The change orders made people on the outside looking in think the team was out of control and ineffective, even though they had improved.

In the end, the new products produced by that team got an ill-deserved, bad reputation by the time they were released. This turned out to be bad news for all.

> ***Based on current measurements,***
> ***how do those on the outside looking in***
> ***perceive the change?***

YOUR NOTES:

21 Challenge Of Change: Assessment

The Trouble With Changing Score Keeping

It might seem easy to change measurements of success. It's not.

It's In The Culture

It's crucial to measure the right things in order to know when and how a change is successful. It's equally crucial to make sure the new measurements of success do not conflict with the old measures. As the old adage goes, "easier said than done".

The system for measuring success in any company has likely taken years to develop and take hold. Over time, that system naturally becomes a way of life. Second nature. The system resides in the forefront of people's minds all the time, and becomes so engrained that they don't have to consciously consider it in order to work by it. The people guide daily activities and spend time in accordance to the established system of measurement. New projects are evaluated based on it. Employee performance is also evaluated accordingly, whether hardwired into the system or just into evaluator's minds. Budgets are set based in line with the established measurement as well.

So when we say that we need some new measurements for success, people may not so easily change. They can change, but to make it happen, plan for the new measurement system, train to it, track it, and line up rewards with it.

> *What measurements have become*
> *a way of life in the organization?*

22 Challenge Of Change: Assessment

Measurement: What The Leaders Need To Do

If measurement and assessment are so tricky, what to do about it?

Measurement Tips

1. **Be patient with the results of change.** Yes, set stretch goals and timelines. Maintain a sense of urgency by continually tracking and reviewing progress. At the same time, be patient with people. That means, be firm but upbeat about goals and timelines. Engage in discussions about what people can reasonably get done, listen carefully to their answers and when it makes sense, respectfully press for just a bit more. Avoid being distracted or misled by the short-term results, by keeping the long-term in mind at all times.

2. **Engage in vigorous debate about score keeping.** Executives and leaders at all levels must be involved in discussions about measurement. Don't cut the debate short just for the sake of time. Dig into it. Listen carefully to people's objections in order to properly overcome them. Continue to present the "why" of how things need to measured in order that people are persuaded.

3. **Get outside assistance.** Partner with a change consultant. Ask for feedback and guidance in order to more tightly link results and rewards to the rest of the change plan.

4. **Open your eyes to every accomplishment along the change journey.** Some of the biggest change achievements may actually be unanticipated, which means that you may miss them if you're not looking. Add to that, to keep momentum high, point to many small wins along the way.

5. **Train, train, train!** Make sure everyone—right to the front lines—fully understands the new methods of score keeping, how they are done and why they are important. This must be done in conversation and coaching as much as in training.

> *How can we see and broadcast wins,*
> *big and small?*

23 Challenge Of Change: Believers And Non-Believers

Some people adopt change early, easily and quickly. Change experts have labeled them "Early Adopters." Like the people who line up to buy the latest and greatest Apple product, Early Adopters take on change with gusto. The Early Adopters may spread positive news about the change that works in your favor. On the other hand, the passion of Early Adopters can fuel communication that is a bit dogmatic and preachy, making the potential converts on the receiving end feel stodgy, inferior and wrong.

Maybe the Early Adopters don't mean to say—or even imply—that potential converts just need to "get with it." But when one is extraordinarily passionate, the other party can easily begin to feel a bit intimidated, inferior and overwhelmed. It's at that point that the believer loses his or her influence with non-believers. This may not always be the case. Sometimes Early Adopters' passion can positively impact those just a bit behind in the change process. Hopefully, that's the case in your organization.

Who are the believers and non-believers in your organization?

How are the believers perceived and received by the non-believers?

YOUR NOTES:

24 Challenge Of Change: Believers And Non-Believers

What Non-Believers Think

And what they say.

As The Gap Widens

Think of the believer versus non-believer gap as you would a generation gap. As the gap widens, misunderstanding grows, and negative judgments spring up like bad weeds in a garden. Each party fails to understand the other. And neither side seems ready to engage in the dialogue that might clear up misunderstandings. You can recognize the non-believers because they say things like this:

- I don't know what management is up to. It's all a mystery to me. I just don't get it.

- Management seems to spend a lot of time in meetings and training and not so much on real work. We get stuck with that. I think they spend a lot of time on pie in the sky stuff. They think they know so much.

- I suppose that now we're just not good enough like we were in the good old days.

- Who can understand what they're saying? It sounds like they're from another planet. There's too much theory and not enough practical stuff for me. Get real.

- They just don't understand us anymore. We are not "in the loop" like we were once. It's like management has their own little cult or something.

What do the believers say? They typically sound close to the opposite:

- How many times do we need to explain? We've been over it all so many times.

- Meetings are important and deserve the time we devote.

- Why do our people resist learning, changing and growing?

- They just keep focusing on how great things used to be. When will they understand that we are not going back? We are going forward!

> *What are the believers and non-believers*
> *in your organization saying?*

25 Challenge Of Change: Believers And Non-Believers

Dialogue: One Answer To The Believer/Non-Believer Gap

Get them talking as a way to clear things up.

Coach The Believers

Your organization can move ahead more successfully with change when the believers become ambassadors for the change, not zealots for it. Train the believers to be great ambassadors from the beginning. Help them understand what to communicate (including talking points), how often to communicate, how to engage in true dialogue, and how to listen to the needs of constituents.

Imagine this scenario. You are sitting in the doctor's examine room. The doctor and the nurse are talking about your current test results, as you sit just feet away. They are huddled together, sharing direct and steady eye contact as they discuss your health, using a language that sounds one step away from gibberish. How do you feel? Odds are, you feel invisible, small, stupid and helpless.

The scenario illustrates the power of communication. In this case, the communication is crafted to separate, confuse and intimidate. How much better might things be if the communication had the power to connect, clarify, and empower?

Train the believers in the skills of dialogue and watch their positive influence grow.

> *How can you coach the believers to be*
> *great ambassadors for the change?*

26 Challenge Of Change: Governance

Who's got the power?

How far can we go? Who's got control?

If the Challenge of Assessment is about "culture clash"—the fight of the old vs. the new—the Challenge of Governance is about "power clash." The questions in people's minds have to do with power and control. Who's got the power and control? What are the boundaries, the limits? Who will make the decisions? How much initiative can we really take?

The traditional hierarchy—with its authoritarian, centrally controlled structure—can have drawbacks in the global marketplace. Typically slower and stodgier, the old hierarchy is often giving way to more decentralized, local control. With new structure come new benefits like a more nimble environment in which decisions and actions are rapid and real-time.

There are also organizations that combine the best of both centralized control and de-centralized control, offering a hybrid of tradition and tomorrow. Such organizations seek to strike a balance of decision-making between home office and the field. In general, the move could be characterized as from dependence on the center—to independence from the center—to interdependence between the two.

The governance structure affects any change dramatically. Account for organizational structure and accompanying governance in order to skillfully plan for change.

> **What is the effect of current structure on change?**

27 Challenge Of Change: Diffusion

Spreading the Spirit of Learning

Diffusion means stimulating a free flow of knowledge throughout the organization, almost as if ordinary boundaries don't exist. Everybody learns from what may have been accomplished in other parts of the company. We eliminate redundancy by openly and efficiently sharing innovations, successes, and leading-edge methods.

When Jack Welch exhorted GE to become "boundary-less," he launched a strategy for diffusion. GE suffered from a lack of diffusion as evidenced by a symptom labeled NIH—short for Not Invented Here. In other words, ideas not invented here have no merit here. Such a close-minded approach leads to limited learning and can be spotted by:

- **Reinventing the wheel.** Someone has done the work before to a very successful end, but no one else knows about it. Or a department of team facing a problem could benefit from work already accomplished elsewhere but don't see how that work applies to their case. In either case, why reinvent the wheel?

- **Superficial investigation.** People go to a meeting, read, and research and but don't dig deeply enough to fully understand the material or idea. Having prematurely concluded that the idea or material "will not work here," they conclude that the fault is in the material or idea, not in those analyzing the material or idea. They write off potentially valuable information as irrelevant: does not apply here.

- **Naiveté.** Naiveté is almost the opposite of superficial investigation. Instead of discarding potentially valuable information, naivete results in implementing an improvement from another area TOO fast, before it's well understood. In naivete, information is used without proper study, planning and guidance, ensuring inferior results and a disappointing lesson in learning.

- **Arrogance.** Some suffer from the attitude, "I know this already." Or "This is nothing new." People suffering arrogance, close their minds quickly to information.

- **Lack of desire to learn.** With this symptom of diffusion, people refuse to investigate new ways of doing things, both inside and outside the organization.

*What barriers to diffusion exist in
your organization?*

28 Challenge Of Change: Strategy And Purpose

Alignment: When Strategy and Purpose Drive Success

Experts say that organizations with superior strategy outperform those with a poor strategy or no strategy at all. So, many organizations engage in lengthy strategic planning processes in order to clarify vision, mission, values and goals. In addition, organizations with a superior strategic plan make sure everyone in the organization can align daily activities with the plan. Alignment is key to execution. Execution is key to getting the plan done.

Alignment is easy to discuss but not as easy to do. Why is alignment such a challenge? There are two reasons.

FIRST REASON: The strategic plan may not be perceived as real, viable and relevant. When a strategic plan is viewed as mere words in a document, with little chance of actually getting done, employees refuse to follow. Just as in any other change effort—and strategic planning is a change initiative in its own right—without the input and involvement of stakeholders, buy-in lags. In some cases, employees have little basic knowledge of the strategic plan, much less buy-in to its value to change the organization for the better. As such, the strategy—no matter how skillfully crafted—becomes a definite challenge of change.

*How does the organization view the
strategic plan?*

*How do those views affect buy-in and
execution?*

29 Challenge Of Change: Strategy And Purpose

More on Alignment

There is another reason that alignment with strategy can fail.

SECOND REASON: Get a head start on aligning the entire organization with the strategic plan by following Henry Mintzberg's (famous organizational guru) advice. Make your plan "emergent" and "crafted" instead of "planned" and "set" (the latter being characteristics traditional planning). Why not just rely on traditional strategic planning methods? For the same reasons that change management practices and tools are so necessary today. Our world is no longer dependable, consistent, or predictable...at least not for long stretches of time. Given current conditions, where the only guarantee for tomorrow is that there is no guarantee, strategic flexibility is the order of the day.

What does it mean to be emergent and crafted? First off, instead of a group of executives traveling off to a posh resort to conduct planning, emergent planning involves the whole organization. Leaders at all levels—along with employees too—engage in discussions about strategic planning. Such discussions, no matter what form they take (and those forms can vary), make planning dynamic and organic, and a process out of which break-through strategies "emerge." The discussions also stimulate learning and buy-in, two conditions that feed robust change. Secondly, to meet the "crafted" characteristic of Mintzberg's formula, discussions about the strategic plan's execution—successes, failures, changing requirements and changes of course—must continue at all levels and through all stages of the planning process. The result? A strategic plan that is reviewed and revised in real time, not carved in stone—crafted, not set.

Who has been involved in the discussions about strategy?

How were they involved and to what end?

Myths Of Change

Persuade people to change their minds and raise the odds of change success. But changing people's minds is as hard as changing their hearts, skills and behavior. If it's true that people resist change, it's even truer that people resist being changed. While the difference seems subtle, for change to succeed, transforming the perception that people are being changed becomes critical. In general, take an approach that helps people feel more empowered and less imposed, which requires lots of communication. As part of the discussion, discuss the common myths and counter-arguments regarding change. Listen respectfully to people's views—positive, negative, and otherwise—in order to discover the myths permeating the company.

With those myths, employ your finest persuasion skills, to include empathy, listening, probing, self-disclosure, and storytelling. Lead with empathy, listening, and probing to formulate messages in favor of change that respond to people's views and don't just counter them. Replace good, old-fashioned debate with inspiration and persuasion.

YOUR NOTES:

30 Myths Of Change:
Transforming Myths Into Realities

Organizations And People Suffer...

Because of the Myths of Change. Know them.

To change peoples' minds about change, start by listening to hear the myths weighing on their minds. Next, help people see that "how they see things" today may not serve them well during change.

Convince them that there is a potentially a different reality—a fresh perspective—that will not only ease the pain of change but can boost confidence and success at the same time.

The benefits of changing views? Increased feelings of strength, confidence, empowerment, control, optimism and hope. For the organization, changing people's minds about change can mean more people who argue and work for progress while the volume on the voice of the victim is turned down.

Think about the myths in your organization.

Which of the myths need to be changed?

YOUR NOTES:

31 Myths Of Change:
#1 Too Many Problems

MYTH #1 – The many problems of this change proves it's not worth the effort.

Any change worth doing ought to show positive results. Problems are proof that the change was not a good idea to start with and are also a bad omen of things to come.

REALITY

Problems are part of all progress and change. But far from being strictly a bad thing, we can learn from problems instead of just suffer from them. The problems of change don't wipe out all of the advantages of it.

In fact, sometimes the problems of change lead to improvements that would not have been discovered otherwise, making what once looked like problems into opportunities.

What are the problems of this change?

What are the opportunities?

YOUR NOTES:

32 Myths Of Change:
#2 Management Is Hiding Something

MYTH #2 – Management is hiding something.

Management must know things they're just not telling. They would rather hide the truth than reveal it, no matter how frustrated we get.

REALITY

It's far more likely that management is sharing all that they know today. Although the anxiety aroused during change begs to be soothed by more information and fewer surprises, sometimes there is no more information to be had and surprises happen despite best laid plans. People will naturally want to know today what is going to happen tomorrow, even when no crystal ball exists. With all the emotional upheaval, it's easy to blame management and become suspicious that they know more than they're telling.

During change it's better to assume that when management knows more, they'll tell more. What looks like a lack of communication or worse, deception, is often management thinking things through, considering new developments, or waiting for more/better information.

What questions do we have for management?

How could we get answers to those questions?

33 Myths Of Change:
#3 Anger Is The Right Thing

MYTH #3 – If I get mad, I can fix things.

Things are screwed up and I deserve to be mad about it. This change isn't going smoothly. My world is turned upside down. There's more pressure than ever before. Who wouldn't be angry? It's the only response that makes sense.

REALITY

Things aren't going the way you like, so you are angry. That's understandable. Maybe you're thinking that if you get mad, you can change things. That's also understandable.

But take a closer look. Is your anger really changing a thing? Has your anger stopped the change? Has your complaining helped to improve things? Have all of your protests done any good?

The truth is, during change things are not going to go smoothly or just the way we want. There will be disappointments, glitches, mistakes and even downright failures. And we will become angry as a result.

But, nursing that anger instead of examining it, or venting anger (blaming) instead of creating solutions, won't yield more positive results. Quite the opposite. Anger that is spewed and spread through the organization is like putting gasoline on a fire. Embers become flames, potentially creating destruction.

So, don't convince yourself that anger is somehow "deserved" and ought to be cherished. Instead use your anger to fuel further discussion not finger-pointing; create a positive solution not revenge; or to energize progress not destruction.

> *What am I angry about related to this change and how can I constructively deal with it?*

34 Myths Of Change: #4 Does Management Care?

MYTH #4 – Management just doesn't care.

If management cared about what we're going through, this change would not be happening. We are being hurt already and will get hurt even more if the change continues. Management ought to care and make things better.

REALITY

Most managers care a lot about their companies and the people in those companies. At the very least, most managers want their companies to succeed. At the very most, they care about how people are affected by change.

Don't automatically assume that managers in your company don't care. Assume instead that the level of care is just not obvious or well communicated. Then, find some managers who you trust, ask for their views, and confirm whether you think management cares or not.

> *What is the evidence that management cares or not?*
>
> *Is this more a myth or a reality?*

YOUR NOTES:

35 Myths Of Change:
#5 Clueless Management

MYTH #5 – Management is clueless and incompetent.

This change is crazy and chaotic which proves how clueless and incompetent management is. If management knew what its doing, things would go much more smoothly.

REALITY

Just because things aren't going smoothly, doesn't mean management is clueless or incompetent. Change is fraught with bumps and challenges and the bigger and more complex the change, the more that's the case.

So, why all the bumps and challenges? By its very nature change demands that everyone must learn, stretch and grow. Everyone, including management, is new and uncharted waters. Far from knowing everything, management people are very much like the rest of us. New and different means they know less than they might like and have lots to learn as well.

Add to that, people who are learning won't perform perfectly at every task, every day and every time. They won't always have answers for every question either. Far from making anyone incompetent, the inevitable mistakes, stumbles and lapses in knowledge are part of the natural price of learning and growing.

What are we asked to learn during this change?

What is management learning as well?

36 Myths Of Change:
#6 Stall Tactics

MYTH #6 – If we stall long enough, this will go away.

If we wait long enough, this change could turn out to be the "flavor of the month." No change required. Everything will just go back to normal.

REALITY

The origin of this myth is reality. There have been plenty of companies with plenty of new "programs" that just don't last. To label those initiatives the "flavor of the month" is true. They fizzled, not flourished.

But just because changes have failed in the past does not mean the current change is going to suffer the same fate. Wait to get on board and risk falling behind with all there is to learn to change. Start now, learn all you need to know, and short-circuit the pain of resistance to change.

Who is stalling and how are they doing it?

How can we encourage the foot-draggers to get moving?

YOUR NOTES:

37 Myths Of Change: #7 Riding Things Out

MYTH #7 – I'll ride this out and do my job just like always.

Some people like to fly under the radar, watching and waiting in the hopes that they'll never have to change at all. They keep doing their jobs the same way as always and refuse to adopt change until it's forced.

REALITY

People who watch and wait don't realize is that they're missing out on some of the exciting action of change. They're missing the chance to learn new things and upgrade their skills. They're missing the opportunity to demonstrate leadership through change. Most importantly, they're missing out on building confidence by tackling challenges head-on.

Watching and waiting may seem appealing as the path of least resistance often does. But the best rewards go to those who take charge of the changes in their lives, not to those who try to avoid them.

How can we persuade the change
laggards to get on board?

YOUR NOTES:

38 Myths Of Change: #8 The Power Of One

MYTH #8 – What can I do? I don't matter!

Whether or not I am part of this change doesn't matter much. I am one tiny cog in a very big system of wheels. So, if I sit this change out for awhile, it won't affect many people or the company.

REALITY

It's tempting to rationalize inaction by insisting that the efforts of one, lone person don't matter. The problem is, it's not true. There are plenty of instances where one, lone person has done things to change the course of history.

You do matter. You contribute something valuable every day, whether you choose to recognize it or not. And your participation in the change matters too. You can add a lot of value by using your skills to be part of the solution, not the problem during this change. And you can add value by becoming part of the progress and an exciting future. When you become more by stretching, learning, and growing, those around you challenged to become more too. Your example will make you a leader, whether you hold the title or now.

How can I become more a positive
player in this change?

YOUR NOTES:

39 Myths Of Change: #9 Why Bother?

MYTH #9 – Changes? We don't need to change!

In a team, department or organization that performs "good enough," change may not seem important or necessary. People enjoy the comfort of the status quo and strive to keep things just as they are. Change may not only threaten to disrupt, it may even threaten to cause pain. Why bother with change under such circumstances? People who endorse Myth #9 tout the old adage, "If it ain't broke, don't fix it!"

REALITY

Really? What about global competition, changing market conditions, demanding customers, and technological advances? These days, wise leaders know that standing still is not an option. We need to change before serious problems, fierce competition, escalating customer demands, and technological advances threaten to make us inferior to the rest. Or even obsolete.

Change is a vital and necessary part of a full life and a successful business. In either case, if you stand still, you may die. If Jim Collins is right—and we think he is—then good really can be the enemy of great. Dare to be great by changing on purpose.

What are the reasons we must change?

What threats does this organization
potentially face or currently face?

40 Myths Of Change:
#10 A Suspicious View

MYTH #10 – What about my job? Am I safe?

"This change looks fishy to me." When people don't understand change, they can become suspicious of it. They wonder about the motives behind the change. They worry about imagined implications of the change, like loss of jobs and budget cuts. And, if those suspicions weren't enough, many people err by treating their speculations as facts, not the guesses they really are.

REALITY

In many cases, the imagined negative consequences of change never happen. There may be some short-term discomforts, like the confusion of learning new things or the disruption of a well-oiled routine. But, far from resulting in grave, negative consequences, what stings today may actually bring very positive rewards tomorrow. As an antidote to becoming obsolete, change may offer the chance to become more skilled and therefore more valuable. Instead of suffering budget cuts, perhaps a team will learn how to streamline a number of things to boost efficiency and reduce necessary resources.

Yes, change poses challenges that frighten at first and maybe even for a while in the future. But those same challenges can challenge people to perform at much higher levels than they ever thought possible. How about using the challenge to learn, explore and grow?

> ***What suspicions thrive during change and what can you do about them?***

41 Myths Of Change: #11 The Blame Game

MYTH #11 – They should be on top of these changes. It's not my job to deal with this.

"They should have this planned." "They should have the answers." "They should know every detail of what needs to happen." "They should know how this affects us." These are the complaints of those who believe the job of change is up to "them," whoever "them" is! Such finger pointers rationalize that it's not their responsibility to make change work and so efforts on the part of change are not necessary. It's all up to "them."

REALITY

No matter who envisioned, planned and started this initiative, you work in this organization and if you want the organization to succeed, it's your change initiative now too. You choose. Better to be part of creating a future along with the rest of the company rather than losing time, energy and opportunity to enjoy the rewards of change because of playing the blame game.

Blame brings everybody down, but when you engage in blame, you become your own worst enemy. You undermine your self-confidence on the inside as well as your reputation on the outside. On the other hand, become a positive part of the change by asking questions, learning new things, and exploring possibilities instead of casting blame, and watch your confidence, competence and power grow.

> ***How have I placed blame during this change?***
>
> ***How can I empower myself through this change?***

Steps For Change

Change is best approached in steps and in a particular order. The steps may not play out in a perfectly linear fashion in real life, but the logical order of the steps on these cards makes change easier to understand, plan and manage.

YOUR NOTES:

42 Steps For Change: The Vision Thing

Step 1: Create the Change Vision

In general, the question is, "Why is this change necessary?" Make the Business Case, which ought to include lots of facts and data, proving the need and the opportunity for change.

In addition, answer the questions, "What is the vision we are attempting to achieve?" In other words, "What will the team or company look like 5 years from today as a result of this change?" Also ask, "What is the Burning Platform that is compelling us to forge ahead?" In other words, what are the significant, negative consequences that we face if we don't change?"

Publish the answers, including facts, figures, data and logical arguments, all making the business case for change convincing. Then, add emotional appeal to make the business case persuasive. Use stories to illustrate the current pain and the prospects for an uplifting future. Craft a vision statement to describe in detail what's coming at the end of successful change achievement.

> *Why are we engaged in this change?*
> *What is the vision?*
> *What is the burning platform?*

YOUR NOTES:

43 Steps For Change: WIIFM

Step 2: Motivate the Troops

To motivate the people who must execute the change—to increase their commitment—imagine what it's like to be in their shoes. Then answer the question, "What's in it for ME?" To answer the question, outline the benefits of change likely to matter most to people.

What's the WIIFM for the people in your company? Tell them how the change will change their jobs for the better. Will the change make their jobs easier or more efficient? Or will the change make them more respected, valuable, and skilled?

Even though the change may create a bit of havoc today, will it ultimately put them more in control in the future? Will it offer people more security, recognition or attention?

And, what if we DON'T change? Then what? Will the losses be big enough—glaring enough—so the employees see how they could lose by not changing? For example, what if we lose market share that might mean lost jobs?

What's in it for the people to support the
change?
What are the answers to WIIFM?

YOUR NOTES:

44 Steps For Change: Prepare The People

Step 3: Train Everyone

Want people to change? Tell them why the change is so important. Set clear expectations, outlining what people need to know and do during change. And then train them to do it.

A major cause of resistance to change is the sheer fear of knowing that we don't know how to do things under the new conditions. Adults who have delivered successful performance until change is introduced face the almost certain fact—whether they are conscious of it or not—that doing new things in the new ways involves mistakes, confusion, inefficiency, and even failure.

Build confidence for performing well during change and prevent unnecessary mistakes by properly preparing everyone. Provide the necessary technical training to support change. In addition, provide change management training in order to explain the change, engage in discussion about it, and teach change management tools.

While you're at it, reassure people that mistakes committed for the sake of learning and growing through change are good mistakes, not deserving of punishment.

> *What do people need to know and*
> *do to fully participate in the change?*

YOUR NOTES:

45 Steps For Change:
Provide Practice, Tools And Resources

Step 4: Provide Time on the Practice Field

Training people to fulfill the requirements of change is a very important step in the right direction, but in and of itself, it's not enough. People and teams faced with the challenge of learning need enough time to practice the new methods.

In addition, they need to know when to stop doing the old and start doing the new. And they need systems and tools to support people's ability to do new things. Even an expertly trained carpenter can't do much without a hammer and some nails, along with practice time to master how to use them.

> *What practice, tools and resources are needed for people to successfully perform during change?*

YOUR NOTES:

46 Steps For Change: Momentum

Step 5: Keep It Going

After the change has been planned, launched and has picked up steam, how to keep the change going? Plan strategies for keeping the momentum high. Answer questions like these:

How will we discover and publish change wins?

How will we know and overcome obstacles to change?

How will we adjust the change plan when necessary?

What are the rewards and recognition for change successes?

How will we gather and analyze feedback from key stakeholders of the change?

What is the communication plan for continuing dialogue with people about the change?

> *How effectively are we answering*
> *these key change questions?*

YOUR NOTES:

Two Dimensions

Leadership literature offers several models that divide leadership behavior into two dimensions: task and people. Task behavior means to provide direction related to tasks: goal-setting, clarifying expectations, training, offering feedback and so on. People behavior means to provide support for people: praising, cheerleading, self-disclosure, listening, encouraging and celebrating. By sorting leadership behavior in this way, developing leaders are reminded to attend to both dimensions. Generally speaking, emphasizing one dimension over the other leaves a leader's approach lop-sided and incomplete.

As is the case for leaders, the approach to change management can also be divided into the two dimensions of task and people. In the task dimension of things, effective change managers build a strong business case and plan for change. In the people dimension, wise change managers conduct the activities that help people manage the transition: communicating, listening, recognizing and so on. Just as leaders can become lop-sided, so can change management. Either the task or people dimensions can receive a lot more attention than the other, resulting in an incomplete approach to change.

YOUR NOTES:

47 Some Stats On Change: Balancing Optimism And Reality

Know the realities of organizational change.

How successful is change?

Vision inspires optimism in the face of challenge and change. But, reality is important too. For a dose of reality regarding change, consider:

- Reengineering initiatives fail 70% of the time (Senge, 1999)

- 64% failure rate among new technological innovations in municipal public service programs (Yin, 1978)

- Change initiatives crucial to organizational success fail 70% of the time (Miller, 2002)

- Major corporate technological investments are not used as intended or are abandoned after 6 months 80% of the time (Gartner Group, 2002)

- Of 100 companies that attempted to make fundamental business changes, only a few were very successful (Kotter, 1995)

- Leaders of the corporate reengineering movement report that the success rate for Fortune 1000 companies is below 50%, possibly only 20% (Strebel, 2000)

- Companies that successfully implement their strategic plans are estimated at 10-30% (Raps, 2004)

As sobering as these statistics may be, don't let them dissuade or discourage you from taking on change. What the statistics do remind, however, is that change ought not be taken lightly. Serious change is serious work, requiring deep and intelligent commitment on the part of change leaders.

As a change leader, to deeply and intelligently commit means to take time to plan the change. In addition, it means getting a consultant or consultants to help guide change, providing direction, input, coaching and feedback. Serious change leaders also engage in lots of dialogue with lots of people on lots of occasions. They move with a sense of urgency but not in haste. They talk about the vision of change—many times and in many ways. They provide the necessary training and tools for change and they keep the momentum going. To commit is to do all of this and more as effectively and passionately as possible and. As a change leader, if you commit, they will too.

How committed are you to the change?

48 Two Dimensions Of Change: Task And People

Pay attention to both. Ignore one or the other at your own peril.

The key activities of any change management initiative can be sorted into two dimensions. There's the task dimension. There's the people dimension.

Task Dimension

What's the business case for change? What is the change vision and strategy? How will the strategy be implemented? How will change progress be measured and sustained?

People Dimension

Do people know why change is necessary? Do they understand the change vision and how it impacts them? Do they know what's in it for them to change? How will we help people through the transition of change? How will we help them manage confidence, motivation and stress?

Two Things to Accomplish:

1. Give equal attention to both dimensions and understand that when change initiatives typically fail, it's because of ineffectiveness in the people dimension.

2. Read the following cards about the dimensions and take the advice.

*How well are we balancing the task
and people dimensions of change?*

49 Two Dimensions Of Change: Task And People

How Credible Is The Change Champion?

Will people follow your Change Champion?

Most organizations that undergo big change assign at least one top management change champion to the effort. Sometimes the champion role extends to an entire champion team. Hopefully, such champions are selected because they enjoy lots of credibility within the organization, ensuring significant leadership influence as well as trust on the part of followers. Credible change leaders are worth following and people know it.

Pick your change champions carefully, selecting them for both strong task and people skills. Then, make sure to poll the troops regularly to find out how well the change champions are maintaining credibility throughout the change.

> *How credible are your change champions?*
> *Liked? Respected? Influential?*
> *Trusted? Competent?*

50 Two Dimensions Of Change: Task And People

A Vision's Not A Vision…

Unless everyone can see it.

After much deliberation and discussion, the vision is crafted. The next question is, "How to get everyone aligned with the vision?" The people must all see it in their minds too in order to do it. Here are some key steps to accomplish that.

1. **Translate.** The vision must be stated in terms everyone can understand. The vague must be made clear. The abstract must be concrete. Metaphors are useful. Examples help. People must be able to see what you're saying, if only in their minds' eyes. One of the finest examples of this is the, "I Have A Dream" speech by Dr. Martin Luther King, Jr.

2. **Plan.** Create a communication plan. To whom will you communicate the vision and in what order? What are the key talking points? What benefits should be conveyed to the people? Who will do the actual communicating and through what channels?

3. **Execute.** Do it! In an ideal change management effort, the entire Executive Team will be prepared to skillfully communicate the vision. The entire team should be able to discuss the vision with the other management and supervisory in order for them to pass the vision on. The rest of the communication plan must be executed as well,

including checking progress and evaluating effectiveness all along the way and making adjustments as needed.

> **What must we do to powerfully communicate the vision?**

Complacency

Complacency:

1. **A feeling of contentment or self-satisfaction, especially when coupled with an unawareness of danger, trouble, or controversy.**

2. **An instance of contented self-satisfaction.**

The connection between change and complacency is a simple, yet powerful one. The more contented and self-satisfied that people feel, the less likely they will be motivated to change. The descriptors—contented and self-satisfied—referred to in the dictionary definition can be equated with the emotional state that exists when one is sitting squarely on one's laurels. A smidgen of arrogance is laced through this type of complacency, and it strips even talented, hard-working, and dependable human beings of their desire to stretch, grow and do more. Why do more when we're good already?

Change management experts say that a sense of urgency for change arises from two possible sources. The first is vision, the force that compels people to look excitedly into the future and then roll up their sleeves to do whatever is necessary to get there. The second is pain and anguish. The types of pain and anguish that fuel change include loss of revenue, impaired reputation and job cuts, just to name a few. In crisis—with its accompanying pain—people move quickly and purposefully to improve what is easily recognized as an intolerable situation.

Both the power of vision and the anguish of pain result in a sense of urgency that suddenly makes people innovative and productive. Under such circumstances, formerly complacent people suddenly stretch and grow without even giving it much thought. In this section of cards, we will explore the danger of complacency to change.

51 Complacency: Identify It

A Prime Enemy Of Successful Change: Complacency

Get change over the hump by identifying and resolving complacency.

Complacency. The feeling of self-satisfaction and contentment otherwise known as: Comfort Zone. Denial. The Status Quo. Blind Trust. Smug. Naïve.

The opposite of complacency is a sense of urgency, an emotional state that gives people a performance edge. A sense of urgency brings the best out of people, fueling achievement, innovation, improvements and the like.

John Kotter wrote a blog describing a privileged visit to Steinway, where he witnessed the building of one of the finest pianos in the world. According to Kotter, building a Steinway takes a year of work accomplished by extraordinarily skilled craftsmen, many of whom have worked in the same jobs at Steinway for 25 years. Ordinarily, one might consider 25 years in the same job grounds for heaps of complacency, but such is not the case at Steinway.

Quite the contrary, workers at Steinway reported to Kotter that they possess quite different attitudes about their work. Steinway craftsman spirits resemble a sense of urgency much more than an attitude of complacency.

- "No piano is ever built the same way twice."

- "I am always learning something new."

- "I work for an amazing company and I'm an important part of it."

- "There is no one else who can do what I do."

What are some examples of complacency and sense of urgency in the organization?

52 Complacency: Define It

Spot Complacency

It's normal and natural...but not always helpful.

Complacency is a normal and natural result of settling into routines, regularly getting good results, and generally performing in a basically good fashion. It's a comfortable state, but also a bit sleepy, where the tried and true trumps experimentation, risk-taking, learning and growing. Complacency depends on yesterday's successes for its potency and erects roadblocks to the kinds of progress that ensures tomorrow's success, so it pays to be able to spot it. Look for:

- The "elephant in the room," meaning a serious issue—on people's minds—yet not addressed; people leave it alone.

- Talking and analysis that become substitutes for decisions and action; preservation of the status quo.

- Execution fails—without notice or confrontation—when decisions do get made; people are apparently not all that committed.

- Strategy gets discussed in the abstract only, minus concrete or specific talk, much less action plans; again, likely an absence of commitment.

- People do not ask challenging or tough questions, appearing to agree; commitment is superficial but scratches the surface and discovers it's not real.

- Discussions are too polite, with an absence of healthy conflict; again, superficial commitment.

- People are not held accountable, meaning performance gaps are not addressed; the status quo rules.

The antidote to complacency? First, recognize it. Then, take action.

> *What symptoms of complacency exist*
> *in this organization?*

53 Complacency: The Flip Side

The Flip Side Of Complacency

Learn to recognize the flip side of complacency too: a sense of urgency.

Experts insist that a sense of urgency is critical to the success of any change. So, what does a "sense of urgency" look like? Look for:

- Serious issues openly discussed. No one walks on eggshells about any subject.

- Talk leads to decisions and action plans.

- Decisions and action plans are executed and when they're not, the failure to perform is confronted and resolved.

- Strategy gets discussed in concrete, specific, real-world terms.

- People ask lots of challenging and tough questions in order to deeply understand the change in all aspects. Those questions are welcomed and are answered.

- Obstacles, pitfalls, and negative consequences of the change are discussed. Healthy conflict is the norm, not the exception.

- People are held accountable for performance throughout the change, although honest mistakes due to learning and growing are embraced and coached.

- People's attention is focused on pivotal organizational issues like the competition, the vision, performance metrics, customers, and the business environment.

> *What symptoms of a sense of urgency*
> *exist in this organization?*

54 Complacency: Look Beyond The Walls

Complacency Buster: Steal Shamelessly!

Jack Welch said it to all of GE. Heed the advice and avoid the "not invented here" mentality.

It's easy for an organization to become too internally focused. The attitude that permeates is, "All that was not invented here, is not welcome here." What a shame! Jack Welch—famous, former CEO of GE—understood the dangers of that attitude. So, he coined a counter-phrase for all at GE to live by.

Steal Shamelessly!

What did Jack mean? Jack was and is a fan of learning, growing, and developing (these days he has his own MBA program). In the case of "steal shamelessly", Jack figured that someone out there has likely done what needs to get done or something close to what needs to get done—before you—and that there's not much sense in reinventing the wheel.

So, why not venture outside the local walls of one's team, department or company and find out how others—hopefully the best and most successful—have done it?

Someone stands to learn a thing or two. And even if what gets done gets done differently than what has been done before, studying how the best have done it is good food for invention. Just remember the second part of Jack's idea.

And Give Credit Where It Is Due.

> *Give an example of how the organization*
> *has practiced, "not invented here."*
>
> *What are 5 ways you could apply*
> *"stealing shamelessly?"*

55 Complacency: Benchmarking

Complacency Buster: Benchmarking

Send them on field trips to discover the best.

Sometimes the outfit we have worn for 5 years—our favorite—does not look outdated until compared with some runway fashions. In the same way, work practices can seem quite fine until compared with the methods of top performers.

Nothing busts the status quo like studying the very best. Purposely test your current practices against "best practices." That's benchmarking.

> *How can you challenge the status quo*
> *by benchmarking?*
> *Who will you benchmark?*

YOUR NOTES:

56 Complacency: The Big Can Fall

Complacency Buster: Even Goliath Can Lose

The bigger they are, the harder they fall.

Shake things up a bit. Share stories about how the mighty have fallen. The business world is full of stories like these. Maybe you have a competitor or two who once enjoyed great success only to fall from that pinnacle. Or maybe there are stories of high flyers who suffered crash landings on the pages of the latest business journals or newspapers.

What is the point of sharing such stories? Aren't they strictly a downer? Not exactly. Stories of the fallen can keep people on their toes, remind them that past success is something to be proud of, but not relied on, for tomorrow's glory. Such stories keep people stretching, achieving, learning, exploring, and growing.

> *What stories about the "mighty"*
> *taking a fall can you share?*

YOUR NOTES:

57 Complacency: BHAGs

Complacency Buster: BHAG For Business As Unusual

Set audacious goals that cannot be achieved from operating "inside the box".

Collins and Porras—authors of *Built to Last*—coined and acronym and phrase: **Big, Hairy, Audacious Goal or BHAG, for short.**

In the successful companies Collins and Porras studied, all employed the BHAG as a strategy. What is a Big, Hairy, Audacious Goal? It's a goal so daring, so challenging, so seemingly impossible, that no traditional organizational practices are likely to support the achievement of it. BHAGs are goals that demand thinking, behaving, and performing "outside the box."

Think NASA moon mission from the 60's and you'll know what BHAG means. Kennedy stated the goal as follows, "landing a man on the moon and returning him safely to the earth" by the end of the decade.

When examined in light of the fact that only about 25% of the knowledge needed to achieve the Nasa moon mission existed at the time the mission was set, the meaning of BHAG becomes even clearer.

What BHAG would challenge this organization?

YOUR NOTES:

58 Complacency: Elevate The View

Complacency Buster: The Forest Or The Trees?

Focus attention on the forest as well as the trees.

"What do I have to do today?" Most people focus on the routine and urgent tasks of their jobs each day. The practical and productive approach of focusing on trees loses its luster, however, when the trees fail to properly support the big picture. During change, aligning people on the big picture—the vision and strategy—of change will enable them to think about more than just "doing my job today."

How to help people align with the big picture of change? Talk about the vision frequently, pointing out how daily activities either support or fail to support it. Tell stories about daily accomplishments that advance the accomplishment of the big picture. Establish measurements based on the overall business process, not just individual functional areas, encouraging people to think about how the work in one area impacts the work in other areas. Set overall business goals, not just functional or departmental goals, and then hold people accountable to those big picture goals. Discuss they types of activities that ought NOT be done, pointing people to new priorities.

What are key activities that
support the big picture?

What are activities that
do not align with the big picture?

59 Complacency: Feedback

Complacency Buster: Feedback From The Outside

Make it an organizational practice to seek performance feedback from outsiders.

One way to combat the tendency to become complacent is to ask for feedback from others. Feedback shines a light on opportunities to improve performance, whether that feedback comes from inside or outside the department or organization.

Like top athletes who strive to continually improve, those who seek to be top performers in workplaces of all kinds, devise ways to get feedback from customers, suppliers, shareholders, and important stakeholders. Ask for bad news along with good news. Compile the feedback and share it with the organization. Discuss the results from feedback at meetings. Use the feedback to imagine novel ways to improve products, processes, services and all else. Create action plans to respond to the key patterns in the feedback. In general, use the feedback to move beyond "business as usual."

What feedback does your organization receive from the outside?

What has been learned from that feedback?

YOUR NOTES:

60 Complacency: Conflict Matters

Complacency Buster: Healthy Conflict

A "too polite" culture is the enemy of progress.

Research reveals organizations that avoid conflict suffer from a whole host of problems, ranging from quality challenges to execution failures and lots of things in between. The fact that people often choose to be polite instead of honest and forthright is no surprise, considering some of the less than desirable consequences of speaking up. Disapproving responses. Being labeled a poor "team player." Aggressive and defensive reactions.

Creating a culture where healthy conflict is the norm is easy to promote as the right thing to do, but it's far less easy to accomplish. Begin by setting an exceptional example of what it means to engage in healthy conflict. Provide training to help people shift attitudes about conflict as well as learn the skills of dialogue. Probe for conflict during meetings by asking for opposing views, bad news, and tough issues. Encourage conflict by listening carefully to opposing views instead of arguing or otherwise punishing them.

How candid is our organization?
How skilled are we at resolving conflicts?

YOUR NOTES:

61 Complacency: Act!

Complacency Buster: Accountability And Action

Wishing is a nice beginning, but action makes it reality.

Breed a bias for action throughout the organization, especially where change is concerned. To keep the momentum of organizational improvement going, insist that a summary of decisions and actions—especially those decisions and actions related to change initiatives—be shared at the end of all meetings. Make sure people are assigned to carry out those decisions and actions.

Then, track the progress of all the plans. When things get done, offer congratulations. When they don't, probe to find out what got in the way. Remove obstacles and roadblocks. Set next steps. Keep things moving in the direction of accomplishing key goals.

> *How effectively is the organization executing change?*

YOUR NOTES:

62 Complacency: The Danger Of Comfort

The Body In The Room

A metaphor for complacency.

A realtor offered this metaphor for change. He explained that when a family moves into a home, it's important to fix things up in the finest fashion within the first six months. Why? After six months, people get used to things—just as they are—no matter how distasteful or unfinished they may seem to outsiders. A pile of boxes in a spare room becomes a part of the room's décor. Unfinished projects start to seem "normal" in their half-completed state and how they might look in the finished state is a lost vision. In the realtor's words, "It's hard to see the bodies in the middle of the living room." The moral to the metaphor?

Momentum Beats Complacency!

So, keep things moving…fast enough…without skipping steps…but moving nonetheless. And, make the evidence of movement obvious to all.

> *How is the speed of change affecting*
> *the effectiveness of the change?*

63 Complacency: Move Forward On Purpose

Are You Ready To Get Run Over?

Keep moving or get run over. Which do you choose?

David Novak, CEO of Yum! Brands admired this quote by Will Rogers. We should follow his lead. "Even if you're on the right track, you'll get run over if you just sit there."

Now, there's a quote to post and follow. Although it may be fine to take a healthy rest from the competitive race now and again, taking too long a break may not be a good thing. When the status quo still works well, use it. But review it often. When the reasons for what worked yesterday aren't relevant today, it's time to make a change. Pose the question—to yourself, to the troops, to everyone:

> ***What are all the things that fall under the heading "that's the way we've always done it?"***

List the answers. Review them. Pick at least one opportunity to change, not just change for change's sake, but change for the better.

YOUR NOTES:

64 Complacency: More On The Sense Of Urgency

The Accidental CEO Speaks...

*Real-world change experiences of David Novak, Chairman &
CEO of Yum! Brands*

The book, ***The Education of an Accidental CEO: Lessons
Learned from the Trailer Park to the Corner Office***, has received
positive comments from many CEOs. What better audience to
herald a book highlighting the work of a fellow CEO? The book
describes some of David Novak's experiences with change at
Yum! Brands. Here's one.

David, like many other CEOs and change experts, talks
of "creating a sense of urgency" around change. He says it's
important, yet hard to do.

David passes on the wisdom shared with him from a consultant
at Pepsi who urged that the way to drive change is to create a
"burning platform." What's that, you ask?

Imagine that you're on an oil rig in the North Sea. The rig
has caught fire. You have two choices. You can jump into the
frigid water and swim to a lifeboat, an option that will be most
uncomfortable and cold, but with high odds of success. Or you
can remain on the burning platform, hoping for the best, a bleak
outlook for your future at best. Which would you choose? Likely

you'll risk swimming in cold, dark waters as compared with remaining on a platform to a fiery end.

When an individual or an organization looks forward and sees uncertainty ahead, it is very motivating if that same individual or organization realizes they are standing on a burning platform. The sense of urgency created by the flames will urge them on, no matter the discomfort they face.

What is the burning platform for change?

65 Complacency: The Power Of Critical Mass

Critical Mass Moves Change To Take On A Life Of Its Own.

The definition of critical mass: a sufficient number of adopters of an innovation so that the rate of adoption becomes self-sustaining and creates further growth. Some organizational development experts call this hardwiring. In other words a change, once temporarily wired, becomes hardwired, requiring little effort to sustain. The electric charge flows at the flip of a switch. Others simply say that a critical mass helps sustain the progress of change.

How do change leaders create a critical mass—the sufficient number of adopters of change—that enables change to take on a life of it's own? Begin by understanding that the followers of change can be divided into several categories: Immediate Adopters, Early Adopters, Later Adopters, Skeptics, and Hardcore Resistors.

Although it may be tempting to win over the Hardcore Resistors at the start of change, research shows that it's far more effective to sway Immediate Adopters and Early Adopters first. Sell them on the benefits of change and sell them well and in turn, they'll sell the change for you. At 25% of the total population, Immediate Adopters and Early Adopters can move a lot of others to change.

Immediate Adopters	10%
Early Adopters	15%
Later Adopters	50%
Skeptic	15%
Hardcore Resistors	10%

How can we convince the immediate adopters and early adopters to join the change movement?

Success Factors

How to increase the odds of successful change? The Success Factors section of cards answers the question by offering a potpourri of techniques and skills from a variety of sources.

YOUR NOTES:

66 Change Success:
Help Managers And Employees

Did You Know?

Those who have researched the phenomenon of organizational change can teach us a thing or two...

According to some researchers, the most critical success factor for change is:

Helping managers be effective change sponsors

What is the next most critical factor?

Helping employees through change

If the research reveals that managers and employees are critical to the success of change, then maybe we ought to focus efforts at helping them through the process. For example, managers may need special training about the change in order to communicate the change to others effectively. Maybe some specially prepared talking points could be part of the training? And perhaps employees could also benefit from being trained about change: what to expect from the change; how to respond during the change; how to get through the uncertainty of change?

How do we help our managers be effective change sponsors?

How can we help employees navigate the change successfully?

67 Change Success:
Small Changes Lead To Big Wins

The Power of 1,000,000 Small Changes

Change does not always have to be big, sweeping, or breathtaking.

Great leaders understand the power of "small changes" and "small wins." Toyota broadcasts the power of small wins through what Toyota calls, "little ups." The mantra?

Little Up, Little Up, Every Day A Little Up!

The Toyota organization implements 1,000,000 ideas a year. That's an incredible number of changes. Toyota accomplishes this through breeding a constant desire to perfect things throughout Toyota. They call it "the Toyota Way." All ideas count at Toyota, no matter where the idea originated or how big or small the idea might be. The Toyota culture endorses the idea of, "Innovate every day in every way!" And alongside that, "Good enough is never good enough."

What sounds good on paper, works even better. Toyota is one of the world's top ten most profitable companies and their culture of perfecting things is the key to that success. One of the secrets of the Toyota Way seems to be that the small innovations stir up less resistance to change.

Add to that, when changes come from everywhere—front lines, middle management, executive level and so on—resistance is also reduced.

> *What are the 'little ups' your department or organization might achieve this month? This year?*

68 Change Success: Good News, Bad News

Looking Reality Squarely In The Eye

It may seem easier to deny reality, but it's better to face it.

Toyota is one of the finest companies in the world. Its rise to the top from its humble, post-World War II beginnings is a fascinating story. The story is so fascinating, in fact, that there are countless books written about "The Toyota Way" and "The Toyota Production System." Who doesn't want to study the very best? Here's one story that offers insight into The Toyota Way.

An American executive joined an American Toyota plant. His many years of experience and superb expertise in the auto industry had gotten him this fine position. One day, the American executive arrived at a meeting of his peers. Of course, he had thoroughly prepared to contribute. When it was the American executive's turn to speak, he launched into a litany of accomplishments. He offered good news, achievements and progress. How nice!

A long-term Toyota executive stopped him short. "Please. You are here with us, so we already know how good you are. Please, tell us about your problems so we can help you solve them."

Did the long-term Toyota exec disapprove of good news? Not exactly. But he most certainly understood that bad news often offers ripe opportunities for change.

What is the current reality of your business?
The good? The bad?

69 Change Success: Be A Positive Model

Mirror, Mirror On The Wall...

Who's the most committed of all?

*"Be the change you wish to see in the world." ~*Gandhi

Lead change as you would lead anything else. Be a great example, first and foremost. That means firing yourself up so you can fire up the rest of the troops.

The spirit you possess spreads, even when you may not realize it, so be honest with yourself.

> *On a scale of 1-10, what is my*
> *level of commitment to this change?*
> *Why?*
> *How can I deepen my commitment?*

YOUR NOTES:

70 Change Success: Attention And Energy

Channel The Energy

During a Shake-up, why not use the energy?

Change shakes things up. Routines are disrupted. Old information becomes obsolete. New knowledge floods in. Priorities are shuffled. Stress levels rise.

If things were comfortable and people were somewhat complacent yesterday, today's change puts everyone on red alert, and hopefully to a good end. People start paying closer attention than usual, wondering and maybe worrying. And no matter how they are actually directing their energy, people are energized.

Great leaders of change use the surge of energy in the most positive ways possible. They realize that as long as people are so tuned into what's happening, leaders might as well help sculpt the view. And, as long as people are energized, maybe it's time to talk, straightening out misunderstandings and making a call to new, constructive action.

The same leaders know that to sit still for long is to fail to take charge of change. In the absence of active leadership, people will use their newly found energy to create their own picture of reality.

They will make up stories about what the change really means, who will be affected and what the implications are for the organization. The precious attention could potentially be wasted on griping, complaining, gossip, and even sabotage of the change efforts.

What are the lessons for leaders? Whether you are a formal leader or informal leader in your organization, take charge of the change, don't be passive about it. Talk to your bosses about the change. Start discussions with others about the change. And as you talk things out, listen carefully, probe to learn more, and when you're pretty sure you've heard it all correctly, agree with what's true (first, building common ground) and clarify the rest.

How can I be a strong leader of change?

71 Change Success: Walk The Talk

Make It More Than Lip Service

Are you walking the talk? A mini-case study

An organization decided to gain a competitive advantage through operational excellence. They decided to pursue continuous improvement, empowerment, teams and problem-solving to reach the ultimate aim. The organization created a vision, made a plan and provided the right training to embark on the journey.

At a process improvement event, one team member—new to the organization—kept resisting the critical analysis of the performance of her area by the process improvement team. Her argument, heard several times by the process improvement team, was "I'm new. I'll have things under control in a few months, after I've had a chance to implement my plans." She became quite a formidable roadblock to the process improvement team's efforts.

What was going on? The new manager is a good person. She was carefully selected for her position. She has lots of experience. But some of that fine experience is within the culture of her past organization.

The culture of her new organization is foreign. She's not yet sure how to act. The new manager believes her career depends on doing things heroically—independently—without the help of a team, despite the fact that her new culture expects something different. Her actions reveal her real beliefs and values—solidified in the old organization—that are going to derail her in the new one.

Smart managers coach people to the attitudes and practices aligned with the new culture. If the organization says "team" then team is how people are coached to think and act. If the organization says continuous improvement, then people must be coached to the attitudes and actions of making things better every day. Align your own attitudes and actions with the new culture. Then ask those around you to do the same.

> *What old attitudes and actions are*
> *people clinging to?*
> *What new attitudes and actions are*
> *expected?*

72 Change Success: Rule #6

Post Rule #6

It's not all about you...

"What," you ask, "is Rule Number 6?" This invention of Benjamin Zander and Rosamund Stone Zander in *The Art of Possibility*, reminds us of a simple admonition: "Don't take yourself so seriously!"

Don't take yourself so seriously! What a constructive shift in attitude for those who take change personally and, as a result, wail and moan about the "unfairness of it all" or "how hard it is" or "it's all just too much." We think it's safe to say that most changes are not made with the persecution of people as the primary aim. So, while it may feel quite personal to people—understandably so—the most positive way to remove the sting of change and roll more effectively with the punches is to lighten up. Don't take yourself too seriously!

It may also help to keep in mind that any well-designed change initiative is meant to propel an organization forward and upward, keeping it competitive and profitable.

Typically, the idea is to find new and improved ways and means to provide superior products and services, taking care of customers and employees in the process, and resulting in exceptional profitability.

As good and responsible as those goals are, they really aren't that personal. If you look at it that way, it's easy to see how Rule Number 6 applies.

How do employees take change personally?

What are their most common complaints about the change?

73 Change Success: Emotions

If It Feels Good, Do It?

How feelings affect change.

Use the model below to analyze a variety of potential changes. The model will help you determine why immediate feelings may make a particular change hard to achieve, even when that change is logically quite beneficial. For example let's say you're a new runner who wants to complete a five-mile run. Which category of the model does the potential change fit? Category 2? Does not feel good but is definitely good for you? Perhaps. The answer really depends on who you are. If you are like many and category 2 fits, plan ways to overcome the immediate bad feelings a five-mile run arouses in order to reap the positive benefits that is also brings.

Class 1 Feels good and is...

- Good for you
- Good for others
- Good for the greater good

Class 2 Does not feel good and is...

- Good for you
- Good for others
- Good for the greater good

Class 3 Feels good and is...

- Not good for you

- Not good for others

- Not good for the greater good

Class 4 Does not feel good and is...

- Not good for you

- Not good for others

- Not good for the greater good

> *How do my feelings—both immediate and long-term—affect change?*

74 Change Success: Involvement

Put People In Charge Of Change

Their involvement is key to commitment.

Ease some of the pain and anxiety of change by putting people in charge of it. Employees who have a say or a hand in the change process feel empowered rather than victimized by change. So, if there are opportunities for employees to serve on committees, plan events, make presentations, offer demonstrations and the like, see that those opportunities are fulfilled. To get people involved in the change, delegate assignments you might otherwise have enjoyed. It will be worth the sacrifice.

What assignments can I delegate?

YOUR NOTES:

75 Change Success: Questions

The Questions Are More Important Than The Answers

Inquiring minds want to know...judging minds think they do know.

Are You Ready to Question?

Cultivate a curious and inquiring mind during change. Doing so will empower you to make informed evaluations, based on critical thinking, not just snap judgments or the popular party line. So, when you hear the latest rumor, ask a few questions.

- What does that mean? How did that come about?
- What is the basis for that decision?
- Where is this decision and course of action going to lead?
- What was the underlying rationale for the change?
- What's the evidence to back the rumor?
- How did they conclude that this will work?
- What are the potential gains? The potential losses?
- And the questions go on...

> *What questions can you ask before*
> *you arrive at answers about change?*

76 Change Success: Worry Warts

Fix It Or Forget It

A technique for you and your team.

Worry has a potentially constructive role in life and work. Constructive worry motivates positive action, correcting a faulty situation. Worry that is not constructive—the hand-wringing variety—ought to be dealt with based on the advice from Anonymous: "Fix it or forget it."

If you're worried about the assignment that's left undone... stop worrying and start fixing it. If you can't fix the whole thing, fix a piece of it. Worry is your signal to act so act now.

On the other hand, if you're worried that management is incompetent and will never be able to pull off the change, consider forgetting it (the worrying, that is). Your worry is not totally incomprehensible or even entirely wrong (although we hope it is), but management's competence or lack thereof is a clearly a worry that you have no control over (unless you're top management, that is). Let it go. Fretting over a situation you can't control is simply a waste of time. No, worse, it is a destructive use of time. Tune in to your worries and analyze:

What can I control?
What can't I control?
Then, do what you can and leave the rest

77 Change Success: Cheerleading For Change

Applause! Applause!

Catch them doing new things right.

Change is hard. That's why it's so important to draw positive attention to change successes every chance you get.

Recognize and reward those who risk doing things differently, innovatively and in line with change. Write thank-you notes. Make public statements. Ask those who are taking risks and innovating to share their stories with the team. Offer tokens that reward the new behaviors.

To start, list the "new behaviors" that support the new culture. Be specific. Make the list as long as needed. These are behaviors to reward.

Then share the list with the team. Ask for reactions. Ask for additions. After thorough discussion, look for positive changes in the way the people perform and let the applause begin.

> *How can we recognize and reward people?*

YOUR NOTES:

Resistance

Far from simply being a headache, resistance can be a force for good. There are almost always really good reasons people push back during change. Wise change leaders transform a knee-jerk tendency to blame resistors—and the messages of their resistance—into an attitude that welcomes resistance as a powerful feedback for fine-tuning change. Such leaders cultivate an ear for the real messages underlying change resistance, refusing to settle for surface explanations. Then, they take their deeper understanding of resistance and install mechanisms to use resistance energy for even more positive change. The lesson of resistance during change is a simple one. Welcome resistance—don't fight it off—and identify the reasons for resistance in order to be better prepared to deal with them.

YOUR NOTES:

78 Resistance: In A Positive Light

Resistance Can Be A Good Thing

Resistance is a good thing? How could that be? To start, experts believe that resistance is the normal and natural result of any change, and as unpleasant as it may seem, indicates that people are taking the change seriously. Equally surprising, those same experts believe that an absence of resistance, far from indicating cooperation, more likely signals a change that is not challenging enough, lofty enough, or meaningful enough to be taken seriously. Or, the absence of resistance may simply mean the troops have become too numb or too burned out to care. Looked at in light of these views, resistance becomes a very welcome force and the absence of it is reason to worry. After all, it takes some passion, some fire, to care enough to fight back.

So, remind yourself that resistance is a positive force for change. See it as a necessary part of change, arising when change is seriously underway. View resistance as a sign that people are engaged enough to care, one way or the other. Embrace it as a potential asset— not just a hassle or a headache—of change.

How do you view resistance?
How might you change that view?

YOUR NOTES:

79 Resistance: Three Common Drivers

Driver of Resistance #1: "I don't know enough."

Antidotes to resistance due to "I don't know enough.": more information; stories of success; charts, graphs, data; briefings; question and answer sessions; detailed action plans; frequent updates; job aids and training of all kinds.

Driver of Resistance #2: "I feel anxious and afraid."

Antidotes to fear and anxiety: more question and answer sessions; listening, listening, listening; reassurance; praise and encouragement; proof of progress.

What won't work? Listening to feelings when the audience is hungry for tangible facts; as well as offering endless facts of change when people are starving to be heard.

Driver of Resistance #3: "I don't trust management."

Antidotes to distrust: deeper dialogue; professional facilitation; trust-building techniques such as transparency and candor; examination of values; disclosing vulnerability through admitting lack of answers or knowledge; sincere apologies for past transgressions that may have led to current distrust.

*What are the drivers of resistance
related to this change?*

YOUR NOTES:

80 Resistance: Top Ten Reasons Assessment

Here is a list of Top Ten Reasons for resistance, compiled from several sources.

1. The risk of change appears greater than the risk of staying the same. *Today's comfort and success trumps tomorrow's vision of change; the leap of faith looms too large.*

2. Change threatens disloyalty to past methods and those who invented them. *People develop loyalty to past practices and their originators; to give up those practices is to break cherished bonds, not only with methods, but with people too.*

3. People may need to see successful change to believe it. *Most people are not visionary; they just can't imagine how the change will work; show them how the change will work via a pilot project or other demonstration.*

4. People fear they will not be able to do it. *People fear that change will require new knowledge and skills beyond their abilities to master.*

5. People feel overwhelmed and overloaded. *People wonder how they will fit the change into an already jammed schedule; when will it all get done?*

6. Healthy skeptics need to be sure. *Some simply have intelligent questions and concerns about the change and want answers.*

7. People suspect hidden agendas. *People wonder whether what's really driving the change has been communicated; or is there more?*

8. People's identities are threatened. *Change may threaten people's identities and therefore, sense of worth (the craftsperson turned administrator for example); in addition, change may alter work enough so that a job once enjoyed becomes less so.*

9. The change will also change quality of life or current status; or people fear it's so. *The supervisor of yesterday becomes the team leader of today and less power and control comes along with the change; or the change changes the environment, the perks, and so on.*

10. People know the change is a bad idea. *Finally, sometimes the change truly is a bad idea and everyone—with the exception of the change initiators—know it.*

What are the most common reasons for resistance in this organization?

81 Resistance: Interesting Facts To Know

Prosci, a company of leading change management consultants, conducts regular research about change in organizations. Here are some of their findings related to resistance to change.

1. The number one reason for employees' resistance to change is lack of awareness of the need for change. *The same reason showed up in managers' top five reasons for resistance as well.*

2. Raise awareness of the need for change by illustrating BOTH the risks of not changing as well as the reasons to change.

3. Ask senior leaders to deliver the case for change. *Employees prefer it. Prosci research proves it.*

4. The most potent resistance managers in the organization are the managers and supervisors whose employees are impacted by change. *This is not a job that can best be done by Human Resources or Organizational Development. Ironically, however, Prosci research reveals that managers and supervisors are the group most resistant to change.*

5. Before supervisors and managers can effectively manage resistance to change, they must become convinced of the value of change themselves. *Do this first and the work of convincing the front lines will become much easier and more likely.*

What are some ways to overcome
resistance?

82 Resistance: Limiting Resistance

Spread the Change Movement Around

Head off resistance to change by getting people's ideas and input, before, during and after.

Want to limit resistance to change? Create a system for getting improvement ideas from all around the organization—including all levels, all teams and all functions.

Make sure to add a method for evaluating and implementing the improvement ideas. Then, report back progress, offering rewards for work well done.

Employees for whom improving things has become a way of life become used to change at the same time. More Change Practice = Less Change Resistance.

How do we get ideas from employees?

YOUR NOTES:

83 Resistance: Involvement

Resistance And Employee Involvement

A proven way to manage resistance: get them involved in change.

Don't simply tell people what to change and how to change. Instead, ask them what changes are needed. Make it part of the organization's routine to get people involved in the change process. Incorporate ways to ask for change ideas during strategic planning.

Create focus groups to gather ideas for change from people. Conduct surveys asking for input to inform change initiatives.

The main questions are:

1. What can we change for the better?
2. What are the most important changes to tackle?
3. How should we make the changes happen?

Listen carefully. Probe for deeper understanding. Take the best ideas and use them. Report the results.

> *How can we get people involved in our organization's changes?*

YOUR NOTES:

Communication

The idea that communication is critical to successful change management is far from new. The trouble is, what kind of communication truly helps? The next several cards offer tips to answer that question.

YOUR NOTES:

84 Adult Learning Principles

Nice To Know Vs. Need To Know

People are bombarded with information at work, at home and everywhere else for that matter. There are countless memos, emails, meetings, books, letters, conversations, directives, and speeches to plow through every day. The sheer volume of information can become overwhelming, confusing, disheartening and paralyzing. Important meaning is hidden in the swirling ocean of data, opinions, and information, but how to discover it?

The best leaders understand the information overload of our times. So, like all great teachers, they tell people what they "need to know," not what people might find "nice to know."

So, if it's important for people to know the time, tell them the time. If the details of how the watch is made don't matter, skip those. At the same time, always keep in mind that you are not the sole, best judge of what defines "need to know". Put yourself in the receivers' shoes and imagine what they might say they "need to know" too.

Finally, put yourself to the test of "need to know" versus "nice to know". Evaluate some of your most recent communications. Ask for feedback from those who you communicate with most often. How well do you communicate what people need to know versus what's nice to know?

What do the people need to know?
What is simply nice to know?

85 Communication

The Communication Plan

Don't leave communication to chance. Plan it!

When the Champions of Change at Motorola started traveling the road to the Malcolm Baldridge National Quality Award some years back, one vital component of the change process was The Communication Plan.

The Communication Plan includes: Who, What, Where, When And How to communicate about change.

At Motorola, messages were crafted. Messengers were identified and prepped. A complete communication system, encompassing verbal, written, visual and electronic communication channels was created. Most importantly, the Communication Plan was executed.

> *What change messages need to be communicated?*
> *Who will communicate the messages?*
> *Where, when, and how will the messages be communicated?*

YOUR NOTES:

86 Communication: Talk x 3

Communicate, Communicate, Communicate!

Experts use the term "over-communicate" to describe how much communication is needed during change. The point of the term "over-communicate" is to emphasize that there can never be enough communication during change. Whatever quantity and quality of information is the norm for your organization will not be enough to inspire and inform people through change. On the other hand, while you can't communicate too much, there is such a thing as communicating too much insignificant or insensitive information. In general, consider multiplying communication strategies by 3 (at least). Talk x 3. That should be a good start.

1. **Share the vision of the change.** What will the organization look like when the change is accomplished?

2. **Outline the logical case for the change.** What business results will be achieved?

3. **Describe what the change will mean to employees**. What will the change mean for employees? How will jobs change? What must they learn? What are the opportunities to grow?

4. **Answer the question for employees**, "If I go along, what's in it for me?"

5. **Outline the steps of the plan for change**. What are the steps we must accomplish to arrive at the vision? Who will do what by when and how? How will we track progress?

Communicate these things many times and in many ways. Use meetings, one-on-ones, presentations, memos, emails, web sites, publications and bulletin boards.

One final tip. Encourage dialogue whenever possible. Employees need to ask questions, offer opinions, voice concerns, make suggestions, and share experiences. Expressing themselves is one way employees take control during uncertain times.

How can we practice communication x 3?

87 Communication: The Power Of Stories

Use The Power Of Stories To Make It Memorable.

Do you have a favorite story from childhood? How clearly can you recall it? Could you retell it? How does the story make you feel? Stories are a persuasive and inspiring form of communication. Stories entertain, make the abstract concrete, and are memorable. They evoke emotions, moving hearts as well as informing minds. It's no wonder that great leaders are often great story tellers as well.

What's more, we all have stories to tell, despite the fact that we often don't know what those stories are. At least at first. When invited to share our stories, however, we can surprise ourselves by telling stories that inspire, motivate and persuade.

Use stories to compel buy-in to change. Tell stories of change success to fire people up. Ask employees to tell stories about change accomplishments to educate and inspire.

Assign a "story of the week" topic and get everyone involved in telling stories of change. For example, telling stories of excellent customer care might be a good story assignment for the week or month. Or, perhaps the team could tell stories of "the best short-cut I have discovered" another week or month.

What stories of the week or month
can we tell to support change?

YOUR NOTES:

88 Communication: Updates

Tell Them The Latest And Greatest

Keep people up to date on change progress.

During change, more information is almost always better than less information, as long as it's information people need to know to successfully change. So, share plenty of relevant information about the change.

Send out change updates via email, bulletin boards, forums, staff meetings, webinars, conference calls, posters and every other communication vehicle possible.

Send the change updates in story form. Tell stories of change successes and failures. Be honest about barriers and how those barriers are being overcome. Communicate change breakthroughs and how those were accomplished. Write articles of commonly asked change questions, along with answers.

Chart progress on timelines spread across walls, complete with artwork, pictures, graphics and the like. Send out data about change as well. Show return on investment figures, quality improvement figures and customer satisfaction stats or whatever other facts and figures might prove the change's benefits.

> *How can we communicate progress*
> *related to the change?*

YOUR NOTES:

89 Communication: Tell The Truth

The Truth Changes

Today's wisdom may be tomorrow's trash.

During change, everything moves so fast and furiously that no one can keep complete and accurate track of every latest development. Add to that, while management operates based on the best knowledge and information of the moment, that knowledge and information changes fast as well. In the end, the best that management can do is to communicate the truth as they know it today. Those managers are wise to add to any message communicated that the truth may change tomorrow...because it might.

So, don't be surprised when what you say and what you hear about the change may change. Help others to understand this phenomenon of change too. Help them to expect that yesterday's message may well have changed by today. Assure them that far from proving that management has lied, such changes in communication during change most often mean that the environment, the conditions, and the requirements demand updated messages. Instead of assuming the worst, continue asking lots of questions of those who are in the know in order to get to some straight answers.

> *You said this yesterday and today*
> *it sounds a bit different.*
> *What are the reasons for the differences?*

And as you share today's truth with co-workers, associates, and your team, do it as accurately as possible. As you share today's message, explain that the truth may change tomorrow, depending on changing circumstances.

> *Here is what I know today. This could*
> *change tomorrow and here's why…*
> *what else do you need to know?*

90 Communication: The Rumor Mill

Recognize Rumors and Respond to Them

Change arouses anxiety, and one way people cope is by making up stories about what's going on.

As a change leader, listen for the rumors and other stories people are telling about the organization's change. Listen for more than the words, asking yourself, "What is the deeper meaning of this story or rumor? What human needs does the story or rumor reveal?" Do people need information? Training? Do they need to know the change benefits? To understand why change is necessary? Once you believe you know what your audience needs, offer answers that fulfill those needs. Educate, inspire, persuade, and/or reassure. Here's how.

Gather the troops. Keep the group size manageable, about 10-20 people.

Ask the group:

> *What are the latest rumors and stories floating throughout the organization?*

1. Write snippets of the rumors and stories on a flip chart.
2. Ask clarifying questions as each rumor or story is related.

3. Conduct voting to identify the most repeated rumors or stories.

4. Offer answers, including facts, in response to each rumor or story.

91 Communication: Differing Views

Invite Differing Views

Assume that others will view things differently than you do…and that it's good.

Conflict is not only inevitable during change. It's a vital part of it. So, the last thing a smart change leader wants during change is to squelch conflict. It's much healthier for the change process to bring conflict to light. How to do that? Ask for differing views. The questions are:

- What parts of my message do you disagree with?
- How do you see things differently?
- What in the change plan should be challenged?
- What are the pitfalls and obstacles we might face?
- What most worries you?

When differing views are aired, listen to them with respect. Don't get defensive. Paraphrase what you have heard expressed. Probe to dig more deeply for understanding. Then, share your candid thoughts, not to defend, but to respond. It's win-win.

> *What differing views might you bring to light?*
>
> *How will you do it?*

YOUR NOTES:

92 Communication: Talk It Out

Talk It Out Or Act It Out. You Choose.

When people experience the loss, anxiety, fear and other messy feelings of change, help them talk it out.

Feelings are messy and often unwelcome, especially in a business environment where people prefer the clarity of logic. Yet, people operate effectively based on having BOTH a head and a heart.

One analogy for how people function is the horse with a rider. The horse functions like the heart: feelings. The horse provides power, strength, energy and speed. The rider functions like the head: rationality. The rider provides direction, steering, focus and discipline. A horse without a rider can run wild. A rider without a horse moves slowly indeed.

To function effectively during change, well-rounded people tune into their own feelings as well as listening deeply to the feelings of others. In addition to identifying feelings, they more effectively manage change by talking things out, not acting them out.

In the absence of talking things out, feelings don't go away. Most often, we act them out instead.

Fear becomes gossip.

Anxiety becomes blame.

Worry becomes procrastination.

Anger becomes sabotage.

Obviously, there are distinct advantages to talking about feelings in order to decide how to constructively respond to them. In short, during change it's better to talk feelings out, not act them out. Acting out results in...

Complaining. Moaning. Groaning. Sabotage. Foot dragging. Back biting. Blaming. Finger pointing. Fighting. Evasiveness. Passive-aggressive behavior.

> *How can we talk feelings out, not act them out?*

93 Communication: Listen Between The Lines

"It's Not Reasonable!"

Learn to listen between the lines.

A call center supervisor posed this question during a seminar. "What can I do when employees tell me it isn't reasonable to expect them to remain calm while customers yell?"

Good question. This call center supervisor is trying to do the right thing by customers. She is promoting great customer service strategies, has set high customer service standards, and has trained the team about how it's done. There is just one small problem. Can you hear what it is?

The Team Gets Tired.

When someone says that what you're asking "isn't reasonable," it would be easy to rely on an old fashioned management style response. "Well that's the way it is and that's the job, so get over it and get on with it." Going back to old management methods misses the point. The employees aren't saying that they're on the verge of revolt. They're simply saying, "We're doing it the way you want, the best we can, and sometimes we get tired. Support us please." The question for you—their leader—is:

Are you listening? Really listening?

*What are some complaints about
change that require deeper listening?*

94 Communication: Communication Test

Apply The Communication Test

So, you've sent the message. How did it go?

Want to know how effectively the message is getting through? Go to the people. Practice what Tom Peters called "Management By Wandering Around." But, wander with a purpose. Learn to ask lots of questions as you wander.

How is the change going? What's working? What's not? What is your understanding of why we are making this change? How is the change affecting your world? What do you think we stand to gain? Lose? What are the biggest obstacles this change presents to you? How can I help you through the change?

Then, listen to the answers. Learn the lessons. Apply some solutions.

> *Who's getting the message? Who's not?*
> *Where are the misunderstandings?*
> *Where are the obstacles? Reservations?*
> *Resistance? Where can we improve*
> *change efforts?*

YOUR NOTES:

Momentum

One of the biggest challenges of change is it's tough to keep it going. Especially during change requiring months or even years of effort, the road seems long because it is long. Obstacles arise. Failures occur. Spirits lag. Skepticism can run high. The biggest and best results of change seem far, far away and may appear almost impossible. So, how do you get momentum going and keep it up once it's established?

YOUR NOTES:

95 Momentum: Keep It Going

Keep It Goin'

Like the Energizer Bunny.

First, check the depth of your conviction. Do you believe, with little to no reservation, that the change is worth pursuing? Do the rewards of change make the risks well worth it? Where you do have doubts—and every intelligent person has some—how have you worked through them?

Change—especially complex, organizational change—is most often a marathon, not a sprint, so shift your attitude to one of settling in for the long haul.

And remember that spirits often lag right before a breakthrough, so hang in there, especially through what seems like the darkest hour.

Finally, look for those who can inspire you through tough times. Post this quote—compliments of Albert Schweitzer—for inspiration:

"In everyone's life, at some time, our inner fire goes out. It is then burst into flame by an encounter with another human being. We should all be thankful for those people who rekindle the human spirit."

Who rekindles your spirit?

YOUR NOTES:

96 Momentum: Roadblocks

Leaders And Managers As Roadblocks

Sometimes leaders and managers have a lot to lose.

And those same leaders and managers almost certainly do not see the WIIFM to change. WIIFM is otherwise known as "What's In It For Me?" So, knowing they have a lot to lose—status, power, control, certainty, tenure, etc.—and being far less clear about what they could gain, these leaders and managers stand in the way of the change. Here's what standing in the way looks and sounds like.

- I just can't get the information from him.

- I offered an idea and she made me look bad to the next department.

- He is supposed to be at those meetings but just doesn't show up.

- Well, we are trying to do this, but she is dictating every move. So much for our ideas.

- He sits and bitches right along with some of the most negative people.

- I did what I thought I was supposed to do and she called me disloyal.

- Empowerment? Are you kidding? He won't let us make any decisions. If we do, he just reverses them.

- Well, we are working for the changes but she keeps telling us it's not how she would do it.

- I get the feeling he wants us to fail.

Some leaders and managers will undermine the change. They may do it knowingly and consciously or they may not recognize their own sabotaging ways (the idea of the unconscious is real). But count on some leaders and managers needing to be coached. Or watch the change die a slow death from their resistance.

> *How are leaders and managers*
> *standing in the way of the change?*

Risk

Only the very naive believe that change carries no risk. So, while you're teaching people how to manage change, teach them about smart risk-taking too. Limiting the risk of change means facing risks first, then planning strategies to mitigate risks as well.

YOUR NOTES:

97 Manage Risk: Pilot Project

The Pilot Project

One way to limit the risk—for leadership, employees and the organization as a whole—is to put the change to the test. A small test. A pilot project.

Choose the pilot project carefully. Try a project of medium risk/high reward. Select a project with good visibility, easily seen by a broad array of people. Plan for a pilot project that can achieve meaningful results. Then set up the pilot project for success by selecting exceptional pilot team players and an accomplished and credible project champion.

Once the project is underway, position it for a stunning roll-out with a remarkable grand opening. Finally, evaluate progress each and every step of the way to learn some of the hardest lessons early, not when the bigger project is on.

What project could we pilot to limit change
risks and raise the odds of success?

YOUR NOTES:

98 Manage Risk: Short-Term Efforts

Focus The Short-Term Efforts

Sure, there may be several strategies that support the change over the long-term.

But perhaps there is a key strategy that will propel change forward with a burst. Identify the strategic element that will ensure the success of change and run a campaign based on that element. Some examples.

Don't Fix Blame. Fix Problems!

Improve One Thing Today…And Every Day.

Get Answers From Everyone, Everywhere.

Don't Reinvent The Wheel. Steal Shamelessly.

Spread the word. Put up banners. Conduct a training blitz to show people how it's done. Publish success stories and celebrate them with lots of hoopla.

What can be your campaign for change?

YOUR NOTES:

Stress

Keep getting feedback about the change, from planning through launch, and all the way through debrief. As part of the feedback, ask questions in order to gauge the stress levels throughout the organization. Why bother?

Stress affects performance, much in the same way that tension affects a violin string. Too little leads to lax performance. Too much results in faulty performance and ultimately, burnout. Just the right amount of leads to top performance.

YOUR NOTES:

99 Stress: Burnout

A Key To Keeping It Going

As the change evolves, it may be tempting to become a more hands-off leader. While things may be going well and change may seem to have taken on a life of its own, leadership is still necessary. The degree of guidance and direction that people need may be somewhat lessened, but leadership through change is always welcome, right through to the end.

So, keep managing by wandering around. Talk to plenty of people. Gather lots of feedback. Constantly search for change successes and problems. Be a cheerleader of change. And, watch closely for signs of stress and burnout. As change evolves and people gain proficiency, you may be able to afford to give less guidance, but your visibility, interest and support will always be a positive force for change.

Who is most likely to be burned out from
the change?
How will we know?
What can we do about it?

YOUR NOTES:

100 Stress: Raise Efficiency

Is This Really Necessary?

One company started a movement to reduce stress and raise efficiency.

The company knew that people were under lots of stress from change. They felt overworked, complaining that there was just too much on their plates.

Management planned a solution. They launched a company-wide initiative to stop doing things. Management set some criteria for what to stop doing to include "things that may once have been useful but have become obsolete." In other words, management was suggesting that the people stop doing anything wasteful, not achieving positive, worthy results.

Each person in the organization was asked to discover things to NOT DO. Yes, in the end, the company created a company-wide Not To-Do List! Brilliant.

> *What are some company-wide ways you can help people keep change going?*

YOUR NOTES:

Quote The Wise

Quotes from those who have achieved great things, are great thought leaders, or just have a way with words, inspire us to examine and improve our lives and work, presumably for the better. This section of cards contains some quotes to lift you and others up during the process of change.

101 Chinese Proverb

Good medicine is bitter to the taste.

~ Chinese Proverb

Change brings inspiration, challenge, improvements, innovation and other fine things. At the same time, change brings uncertainty, anxiety, fear, mistakes and maybe even failure. The mix, as is also true in much of life, is both good and bad.

What is the bitter medicine that some will have to endure as the change unfolds?

102 Chinese Proverb

*Trees may prefer calm but the wind
will not subside.*

~ Chinese Proverb

Yes, we all enjoy the security, safety, comfort, and peace of the status quo. No matter how much we enjoy the stability of the status quo, change is inevitable. Change will happen. Learn to embrace it when it does, and learn to manage it to the best outcome for you and everyone around you.

*How can I embrace the changes
in my life and work?*

103 Victor Hugo

There is one thing stronger than all the armies in the world, and that is an idea whose time has come.

~Victor Hugo

You may not want change, but an idea whose time has come will over-power you, despite your best efforts to resist. Turn your energy to in a positive direction just like Kenny Babyface Edmonds. Kenny shared with Oprah, that when his first response to adversity or challenge is to turn away, he purposely does the opposite. "I embrace it." he said.

What is a challenge to embrace?

104 Winston Churchill

The price of greatness is responsibility.

~Winston Churchill

Every moment of life and work offers a decision. We choose to take accountability for what faces us. Or we choose to complain and blame.

Each time you choose accountability, your strength grows. Each time you complain and blame, your confidence wanes.

Choose strength. Choose power. Choose accountability.

How can I take charge of this change and therefore, be accountable?

105 Napoleon

The responsibility of the leader is to
define reality and create hope.

~Napoleon

Learn to look at the way things are. And talk about the way things are. Good stuff. Bad stuff. All the stuff. Learn to shift your eyes to the possibilities of the future and talk about that as well. GREAT STUFF! The Future Stuff. The mantra is:

We Will Get There And It Will Be Glorious!

> *What is the reality?*
> *What is the hope?*

106 David Novak

I've come to realize that one of the biggest gaps in business, as in life, is the knowing versus the doing. We knew what to do, we just had to get better at getting it done. Customer mania and execution are now THE major themes for our company.

~David Novak, Chairman & CEO Yum! Brands

David Novak has learned the lessons he speaks of firsthand . He tells the Yum! Brands change story in his book *The Education of an Accidental CEO: Lessons Learned from the Trailer Park to the Corner Office. We can all enjoy David's lessons learned.*

What do you know but not yet do?

How can you close the gap?

107 Henry Adams

The law of nature is change
while the dream of man is order.

~Henry Adams

So it goes. We seek order in this seemingly crazy, messy, chaotic world. Some of us seek order more fervently than others, but we all seek it. And yet, as Henry Adams reminds us, life is messy.

Messy is the way things are meant to be. We can continue to seek order, but at the same time, dare not forget. Some of the most exceptional achievements of history have been born out of chaos, risk-taking, experimentation, and trying things. Progress is chaotic more than it is orderly.

How much do you crave order?
How well do you respect chaos?

108 Alexander Graham Bell

Sometimes we stare so long at a door that is closing that we see too late the one that is open.

~Alexander Graham Bell

Looking back. Reflection. Sentiment. These are all good things. History teaches us much and often touches our hearts as well. Fine. But, let's look forward as well. If you spend too much time looking in the rearview mirror, you may miss the possibilities ahead.

What do I want to be doing in this company in five years?
What is my role in this change?
What are some of the possibilities facing this industry?

109 Chinese Proverb

It is easy to dodge a spear you can see, difficult to guard against an arrow shot from hiding.

~Chinese Proverb

We have choices as leaders. We can know what people think because we have asked and listened. By doing so, we can dodge spears with intelligent answers and positive actions. Or, we can guess what people are thinking. Worst of all, we can pretend that what we don't know won't hurt us. The arrow in hiding can hurt us. We are better off to know what's on people's minds and in their hearts related to the change.

What are the spears to dodge during this change?

110 Faith Baldwin

Time is a dressmaker specializing in alterations.

~Faith Baldwin

Oh, how lovely all might be, if plans unfolded exactly as written! What security. What a sense of control.

We make plans to change carefully plan to get things right. We figure out ways to enlist the help of others, avoid pitfalls, and gather resources.

We count on change plans and too easily forget that plans are just a tool, not a guarantee.

How do you react when your change plans change?

111 Eric Hoffer

*In times of change, the learners inherit the Earth,
while the learned find themselves beautifully
equipped to deal with a world that no longer exists.*

~Eric Hoffer

The best organizations are filled with people who love to learn. No, they are not exactly and automatically learned people. But they are learning. Learning organizations go to great lengths to offer a variety of ways to learn, grow, develop. Classes. School. Coaching. Online learning. Mentoring.

*How is learning encouraged in this
organization?*

112 Charles Darwin

It is not the strongest of the species that survives,
nor the most intelligent,
but the one most responsive to change.

~Charles Darwin

A powerful way that people can become more responsive to change is to cultivate the ability to see issues from a variety of perspectives. Responding to change requires an ability to shift views.

What are the common views of the
current change?
What are some other perspectives?

113 Unknown

People don't resist change.
They resist being changed.

~Unknown

It's hard enough to change according to one's own wishes. Even the person who wants to quick smoking very badly will find it hard to quit. Imagine how much harder it will be to change when it's someone else's idea? Likely very hard.

People resist change in general, for many reasons. They resist being changed even more.

How does our organization help
people overcome resistance?

How do I help people overcome
resistance?

114 Admiral Grace Hopper

If it's a good idea, go ahead and do it. It is much easier to apologize than it is to get permission.

~Admiral Grace Hopper

In strong and savvy teams and companies, people do communicate often and clearly about what is being done. By the same token, those strong and savvy teams and organizations know that forging ahead may mean moving immediately and quickly, before every single person can hear the message in full detail.

That is how the entrepreneurial, agile culture works. If that's the culture you want, make sure everyone knows it's better to act than stand still. It's better to be candid, not just gain approval. And it's better to ask for forgiveness rather than permission for the sake of taking initiative for change.

> *How do you take initiative at work?*
> *How easy or difficult is it for people to*
> *take initiative in this team or company?*

115 James Baldwin

Not everything that is faced can be changed. But nothing can be changed until it is faced.

~James Baldwin

Bossidy and Charan wrote a whole book about it. *Confronting Reality: Doing What Matters to Get Things Right* is dedicated to the idea that unless people ask challenging—even piercing—questions about the current reality, the juiciest future opportunities can easily be missed.

Despite this truth, in too many organizations, too many people cover things up instead of opening them up. They spin it rather than saying it straight. They shift blame, not taking responsibility for how things are. And they stay silent, hoping for the best, not pitching for it.

Want to build a strong culture? Build it on truth, not appearances.

> *What are some of the truths of the organization?*
> *That everyone knows but no one talks about?*

116 Anonymous

Leaders manage change. Managers control process.

~Anonymous

The root meaning of the word Lead is "to go." The root meaning of the word Manage is "to control." Organizations need both. The best leaders do both. They go places in order to reach new destinations, discover new products and services, develop new markets, and revamp processes. And they control what requires consistency and predictability, clarifying process requirements, tracking budgets, and managing projects to name just a few.

What is one key to the healthy and thriving organization? Know when to lead. Know when to manage.

When do I need to lead?
When do I need to manage?

117 Peter Drucker

Every organization must be prepared to abandon everything it does to survive in the future.

~Peter Drucker

Drucker says it well. Nothing done by the people, team or organization—no matter how wonderful that thing may be—is sacred. Everything can be improved and must be improved.

But in the most literal sense, organizations do not abandon things of the past for things of the future. People do. Organizations that progress have created people who progress, actively searching for ways to chuck the status quo in favor of far better ways of doing things. People like that have learned to take pride in doing the new as well as the old. They are people who don't settle for "if it ain't broke, don't fix it."

How well prepared are people to change things?
Improve things?
How can we better prepare them?

118 Anonymous

If you don't create change, change will create you.

~Anonymous

It's easy to settle into what's working. Some people even endorse "if it ain't broke, don't fix it." as an effective way to operate. With that philosophy in mind, people are not likely to make change until it's forced. The forces can be painful:

Competition that takes a good share of our customer base.

Higher priced supplies resulting in compressed margins.

The best talent leaving our organization for another.

Our core product or service becoming obsolete.

The smartest people and organizations do not wait until conditions make anything less than change impossible. They take charge of change. They look for ways to improve things— on purpose.

What are you doing now that falls under the heading, "that's the way we've always done it?"
Where are the opportunities to take charge of change?

119 Unknown

Change is the essence of life. Be willing to surrender what you are for what you could become.

~Unknown

It's easy to get attached to "This is who I am." A solid sense of identity is comforting, providing security and even a sense of pride. We convey this identity in statements like:

I am one of the guys first, above all else.

I've put 25 years into this profession and remember what it was like back then.

I like control. That's just the way I am.

Change challenges us to grow, adding more to what we are. We may not have to exactly give up everything we have worked for and consider part of our identity, but we will have to make room for the new to exist alongside the old.

What strengths and talents have paved the way to success today?
What strengths and talents must be cultivated to ensure success tomorrow?

120 Mahatma Gandhi

Be the change you want to see in the world.

~Mahatma Gandhi

If you want to see change in others, the team or the organization, adopt the mantra, "If the change is to be, let it begin with me." Become an impeccable role model for the kind of change you desire. Then walk the talk consistently, over time.

What changes would you like to see in the team or organization?

How can you "be" one of those changes?

121 Ralph Waldo Emerson

For everything you have missed,
you have gained something else,
and for everything you gain,
you lose something else.

~Ralph Waldo Emerson

People, teams and companies embark on a path of change to achieve gains like more money, better health, new products, heightened spirits, improved profits and the like.

The possibilities for change rewards are endless and exciting. What is sometimes overlooked is the fact that with gains come losses. And people react to losses of all kinds—even those that are the result of planned change—with grief.

What are people losing during change?

122 Leo Burnett

When you reach for the stars,
you may not quite get one,
but you won't come up with
a handful of mud either.

~Leo Burnett

Progress can be frightening, even when it's planned and chosen. Deep down we know that constant and consistent success is not guaranteed. At the same time, life and work without "reaching for the stars," now and again, takes us nowhere. That IS guaranteed.

So reach for the stars. No, success is not guaranteed. But, learning, growing, and stretching are.

What stars can you reach for?

123 Walter Benjamin

These are days when no one should rely
unduly on his competence.

Strength lies in improvisation.
All the decisive blows are struck left-handed.

~Walter Benjamin

Yesterday's success does not guarantee success today or tomorrow. On a more personal level, the skills made you successful once upon a time, may not be the skills that will ensure success going forward.

Enjoy reminiscing about past successes, but challenge yourself to grow for tomorrow.

What are the ways you can grow?

What are the ways the team
or organization can grow?

They believe that nothing will happen because they have closed their doors.

~Maurice Maeterlinck

Sometimes looking the other way means problems disappear. But more often:

- Closing the door on problems does not make them disappear.

- Avoiding a tough conversation does not resolve an issue.

- Minimizing a difficulty does not diminish its consequences.

What is a problem you have closed the door on?

To what end?

125 Mary Pickford

You may have a fresh start at any moment you choose, for this thing that we call 'failure' is not the falling down, but the staying down.

~Mary Pickford

Are you afraid of making a mistake? If so, you're not alone. That likely means you are conscientious, careful, and thorough. You probably have lots of good work habits.

But the fear of making mistakes, which is especially prevalent in those who have good work habits, makes those same good performers shy away from change. After all, making change guarantees a certain number of mistakes.

The idea that a mistake makes a person incompetent, or bad, or wrong is the only things that's really wrong with mistakes. That, and the fear of change is creates. Build your confidence about change and the fact that you may stumble along the way of progress. As Mary Pickford says, falling down is not the problem. Staying down is.

What are you avoiding because of fear of failure?

CONCLUSION

We hope you found this journey as inspiring as we did. Change is challenging for everyone, even for those who embrace change whenever possible. The important thing to remember is that we all suffer during change but it can be a rewarding experience if you let it.

We know that change efforts can fail. But using these cards can help you get beyond the potential of failure and be successful. Use the cards to help you ask the tough questions.

Use the cards daily and with others in the organization. Your dialogue will help your organization to identify the pitfalls and plan for successful change. It doesn't happen by accident—you need to question and delve deep into the resistance to change. Only then can you provide the support that people in the organization need for the change to be a success.

We wish you the best of luck with your change process.

Chris and Deb

YOUR NOTES:

PICK A CARD...ANY CARD

How to use WOW! Change Cards? Let us count the ways. Here are just a few ideas. Use these ideas to get started. But don't limit yourself. Put on your creative hat. Invent some new and novel ways to use WOW! Change Cards and then tell us what you did.

Ideas For You

Display the cards on your desk. Focus on one card per day. Read the card several times during the day. Reflect on what the change lesson means to you. Start a change journal and write your answer to the discussion question.

On the move? Take WOW! Change Cards with you. Or, carry one card at a time. Put that card on your mirror or car visor or anywhere in easy view. Read the card several times during the day. Reflect on what the change lesson means to you.

Not a very methodical person? No matter. Pick your "daily dose" of change from anywhere in the WOW! Change Card deck. The fun is in the surprise. Read the card several times during the day. Reflect on what the change lesson means to you.

Start with the big picture. Scan the whole WOW! Deck. Make note of the most interesting or relevant sections. Use those cards first. Do the others later, based on interest or need.

Scan the WOW! Deck, looking for 3-5 lessons to reinforce recent change training that you attended. Post or carry those cards as reminders of what or how to apply on the job.

Ideas For Meetings and Teams

Display the WOW! Change Cards in the center of your meeting room table. At regular staff, department or project meetings, ask a participant to pick a card, either from the front of the deck or from anywhere in the deck. Ask another participant to read the card. Lead a discussion of the question on the card.

Want to involve more people? At the end of this meeting, ask for a volunteer to select a change card for the next meeting. Put that person in charge of leading the discussion. There will be plenty of time for him or her to prepare between this meeting and next.

Have a larger meeting? Break the large group into smaller groups (5-6 participants per group is nice). Ask each group to pick a card, read it, and discuss it. Have plenty of time? Ask small groups to report back key points to the large group.

Variation 1...select discussion cards before the meeting. Choose cards most relevant to your particular change initiative.

Variation 2...Assign the same card to each small group. Ask each small group to report to the large group. Compare the key points from each small group's discussion.

Do a reality check. Ask participants to discover real-world examples of the change card concept or idea in successful action.

Or failing. Make the assignment at this meeting, giving time to gather real-world examples before the next meeting.

Play a change game. Pass out change cards to meeting participants. The cards can go to individuals, pairs or small groups. Ask each card holder to study the card. Then, each must apply the card lessons BETWEEN the current meeting and the next. At the next meeting, all can compare notes about experiences applying lessons.

Do a change assessment. Pick up to 10 WOW! Change Cards. Divide the meeting participants into pairs or small groups. Give the "10 pack" to each set of pairs or small group. Ask each pair or small group to assess the effectiveness of change in each of the 10 pack areas. Each should report discussion results.

Variation 3...No time to assess and report this time? Make the assessment assignment today and ask for reports at the next meeting.

Variation 4...Instead of a "10 pack," give each pair or small group fewer cards. Even one card will do.

Variation 5...Instead of pairs or small groups, ask individuals to do the assessment and report results.

Variation 6...Set an assessment scale such as 1-10; 1 = poor 10 = excellent. Ask for reports that offer both an assessment item rating and explanation.

Ideas For Training

I. Get Ready For Training

Use WOW! Change Cards for classroom training preparation. Give each participant a deck of cards for the pre-training work. Ask participants to select 3 cards before coming to training. One card should describe a success or strength of the organization during change. One card should represent a change challenge of the organization. The third card should represent one question the prospective trainee would like to have answered. Ask for cards to be shared during training introductions or during strategically placed small group sessions.

Shorter training? Ask for just one card to be selected during pre-work. Hear about the cards during introductions or during a small group activity.

Variation 7…Ask participants to search for real-world examples illustrating the card of their choice. The examples can illustrate successful change efforts by the organization. Or, the examples can show where the organization can improve change efforts.

Variation 8…Ask prospective training participants to choose one WOW! Change Card that you would like him/her to present during training. The presentation can be simple. Read the card. Comment on the card. Offer a real-world example of the card's lesson. The real-world lesson could be personal as well as professional.

Ask participants to pick a WOW! Change Card to share with his/her team, department or colleagues. Ask each participant to bring comments from those people to class, along with comments about change management in the organization.

II. Rev-Up Classroom Training

Use WOW! Change Cards to start training with a bang. Make introductions interesting and worthwhile. Have each participant draw a card randomly from the deck (this would be particularly good with the Wow! Change Card Volume 5, Quote the Wise). Ask the participants to consider how the card relates to each of them and share that in the introduction.

Use the WOW! Change Cards for small group discussion. Ask each small group (2-8 participants) to select a card randomly from a deck. The small group should read and discuss the card. They should then report key points to the whole class.

Variation 9…Each small group should receive the same card so discussion results can be compared across the whole class.

Variation 10…Each small group will receive a card or several cards to read. Then, ask the small groups to discuss how effectively the organization fulfills the requirements of the card, with examples as evidence.

Variation 11…The assessment might include a rating scale of 1-10; 1 = poor, 10 = excellent. Each group should offer a rating for each card along with comments and examples.

Create discussion tables. Assign a facilitator for each table. Ask small groups to rotate from table to table. The facilitator should remain at the same table for all discussions. Each small group should add to the discussion notes during each round. Facilitators should share and post results at the end of the small group discussions.

Energize the group. After participants return from a break, share a card and ask for several brief comments before digging back into the agenda.

Conduct a group grope (Yes, we said "grope"). Pass out 3 cards to each participant. Ask them to mix for 10 minutes, comparing cards and trading cards when they wish. Ask them to talk with as many people in class as possible during the 10 minutes. Put some cards on a side table for additional trades (go to http://www.thiagi.com for more information on Group Grope).

Give a deck of cards to each small group of 5-8 participants. Ask each small group to select 5-10 cards that they find most interesting. Ask them to discuss why those cards draw their attention. Then, ask them to prioritize the cards according to level of interest or importance. Each group should report their results to the class.

Use WOW! Change Cards for classroom transitions. Before breaks or at the end of a training day, ask small groups to select a card that captures a key learning point. Ask each group to share the card and why they chose it.

Break up the classroom action by asking a participant to choose a WOW! Change Card from the deck. Take a few minutes to read and discuss the card before moving to the next agenda item.

III. Make Training Stick!

Reinforce training concepts, ideas, and actions by sending a WOW! Change Card deck with each participant. Explain how to use the cards for on-going learning after classroom training.

Ask training participants to submit a post-training report about how each used a change concept or idea in life or work.

Pick a WOW! Change Card that each participant should read and review after training. Ask that the participants submit an email or internet/intranet report explaining how he/she used the card concept or idea.

Send each training participant a WOW! Change Card each week for at least six weeks. Ask for feedback about how each participant has used the card concept or idea.

YOUR NOTES:

HOW ADULTS LEARN

You work with adults. And effective change depends on learning. Lots of learning. So, it pays to know how adults learn. Here are the principles that—when skillfully applied— the learning gurus say create strong learning environments and experiences for adults.

To begin, realize that adult learners have special needs. Adults receive information from each of the five senses. Take a look:

- 83% of information from what we See

- 11% of information from what we Hear

- 1% of information from what we Taste

- 1.5% of information from what we Touch

- 3.5% of information from what we Smell

Get the picture? TELLING people what to do isn't effective. SHOWING them what to do works much better. (Are you surprised that "smell" outdid "taste" and "touch"?) And, to teach so it sticks, use all of the senses. In addition, apply these adult learning principles:

Adult Learning Principles:

Reinforce It!

Adults do what is rewarded. In training, give lots of chances for people to answer questions and then reward their answers. Even an affirmative, encouraging look is a reward worth offering. Or, pass out token-type rewards like pieces of candy.

Emotions Rule

Boredom is out. When their eyes glaze over, liven things up. Tell a story. Ask them to tell stories. Share a joke. Play a game. These methods make it easy to learn new information and anchor the information with the power of emotion. Voila! Learning that sticks.

Be Active, Not Passive

Make training active, not passive. Ask questions. Encourage them to ask questions. Answer questions. Question their answers. In short, training—like great communication—is a meeting of the minds. It's best when it goes both ways. The good old-fashioned information dump just doesn't work.

Practice, Practice, Practice

Top performers get to the top by lots of practice and feedback. Ask participants to talk about what they will do with what they've learned. Ask them to create action plans for application following training. Give them real-world scenarios to role play. Conduct fishbowl sessions so the larger class can comment on the practice efforts of a smaller part of the class. Create simulations that test principles and practices acquired during class or e-learning.

Link the Old with the New

Find out what the participants already know that can help them learn new material. Mine participants' experiences by asking questions and listening carefully to answers. Ask questions that elicit full descriptions, similar to behavior-based interview questions. For example, ask "Tell us about a time when you were treated differently than everyone else in a group setting? How did it feel?" Or, "Everyone faces significant change sometime during life or work. Tell us about a time when you faced significant change. What happened? How did you handle it? What were the results?" Then, link past experiences with new material, making it easier to digest, understand and stick.

Different Strokes for Different Folks

Different people learn in different ways. Smart trainers know this and plan learning experiences that appeal to different learning styles. For example, ask participants to write, talk, draw, and act. Ask them to learn individually, in pairs, in teams and online. Shake things up with a variety of ways and means for learning.

Get Real!

Adults prefer to learn what they NEED to know as opposed what is NICE to know. So, provide less theory and more nuts and bolts. Related to that, adults thrive on learning the knowledge, skills and abilities necessary to do the job tomorrow, or at least soon thereafter. Give participants the important skills and let them practice, so they're prepared to go out and do.

Some More Specific Tips

Those are the main adult learning ideas to consider. Now, for a few more specific ideas...

Keep it practical and help people solve real problems.

- Use examples and stories to make concepts real, tangible, and practical.

- Encourage discussion about how learning will be used.

- Enhance learning through collaboration. Plan for lots of talk with peers.

- Discuss how the learning may be hard to apply. Ask, "What are the barriers and potential stumbling blocks to using this material?"

- Ask, "What are some problems this material will help you solve?"

Catch them doing things right, as often as you can. Prepare learners for success.

Provide ways to practice new skills and discuss practice results throughout the learning experience.

- Help learners become more and more successful, one step at a time.

- Give clear expectations for each practice round to boost confidence.

- Reward and recognize successes, small, large and in-between.

- Ask, "How can we help you succeed?"

Go back to go forward.

- Ask participants to share past experiences that may be relevant to new learning.

- Pinpoint participants' learning needs. Ask for input about the agenda.

- Adjust the timeframes on the agenda to fit participants' needs.

- Ask participants what they really need to know about a topic.

- Quickly adjust to learners' needs by being a flexible trainer.

- Design follow-up support for learners as they apply new knowledge and skills; i.e. a learning help line.

- Ask, "How can we best support your ability to apply what you've learned to the job?"

Establish a safe and respectful learning environment.

- Make learners physically comfortable during the learning experience.

- Be well organized and make good use of learning time.

- Avoid big words and jargon. Don't "talk down" to participants.

- Validate learners' views even when offering a different perspective.

- During class, frequently ask for feedback about how the learning is going.

- Get input to enrich the learning experience.

- Ask, "How can we make this learning experience the best you've ever had?"

Provide choice and alternatives to fully engage the adult learner.

- Show learners the gap between what they know today and what they need to know tomorrow.

- Share your agenda and ask for reactions and input.

- Discover what the learners know about the topic already.

- Ask what they would like to know about the topic.

- Create a learning plan with a variety of learning methods.

- Incorporate action-planning time into the learning agenda.

- Ask, "What will you do with this when you get back to work?"

Skills For Facilitating Learning

In the old days, managers gave answers. Workers used those answers. Times have changed. These days, the smartest managers are teachers. They want the employees to have the answers or to discover their own answers. So, those managers facilitate learning instead of dispensing answers like pills from a bottle. The old job description of "manager as know-it-all answer provider" no longer applies.

WOW! Change Cards offer a juicy opportunity to facilitate learning, helping people find their own answers, instead of just dispensing them. And during change, peoples' ability to learn is a key ingredient to success. It doesn't do much good to order people to "CHANGE ALREADY!" It's much better to engage in training—both formal and informal—about why the change is necessary, what might be achieved, what problems might occur, how things will be tackled and what everyone stands to gain.

WOW! Change Cards are structured to support on-going, day-to-day learning. In addition to some content, most cards have a question or two to get people thinking and talking. By using the cards—with the questions—executives, managers, supervisors, project managers and team leaders can easily facilitate learning. And employees can take charge of discovering the best answers.

Here are some methods for facilitating learning. There are also learning methods on some actual WOW! Change Cards, but the ones included here build on those ideas. Use any of the methods, whether you are a bona fide trainer or a change leader who is taking your new role as facilitator of learning to heart. Use one. Use several. Over time, you may use all the methods here. Enjoy!

Get Them Involved And Keep Them Involved

Ask for volunteers: to present, to report, to ask a question, to pose a challenge, to keep track of time.

Make a job jar. Fill the jar with roles that must be fulfilled during the meeting or training. Ask people to draw a job from the jar and do that job for the day. Rotate jobs at each session. Job examples? Time keeper, devil's advocate, summarizer, recorder, comedian, story-teller, interviewer, and the like.

Get frequent feedback. About the subject, issues, opinions or anything else related to the topic at hand. Ask for a simple "thumbs up" or "thumbs down" on a topic, idea or opinion. Or, pass out sign cards—"+," "-," "?"—to get instant feedback. Use symbols to get the kind of quick, yet accurate feedback you want. These days, you can achieve the high-tech version of gathering feedback using Twitter and PowerPoint technology.

Post a flip chart for feedback. Tell participants to write comments on the page throughout the meeting or training. Comments might include what's liked, what's disliked, ideas for follow-up, questions and so on.

Pose pre-meeting or pre-training questions and ask participants to come prepared with answers.

Ask participants to come prepared to share real-world situations that they would like to have addressed.

Use stories and quotes to start sessions with a bang. Ask each participant to share what a particular quote means to him or her. Ask each participant to share a story that relates to the subject at hand. Or, use a quote or story from a WOW! Change Card deck to start a lively conversation. (Stories are included in Volume 4-Inspiring.)

Assign a question and ask pairs to interview one another using that question. Ask for answers from each pair.

Give them journals. Encourage participants to take notes during each session. Ask them to emphasize action. What will they do as the result of the meeting or training?

Conduct a question and answer session. Ask participants to pose a question on an index card. Collect the cards. Shuffle and pose several questions to be answered during the session. Or, redistribute the cards and ask for answers in writing.

Do frequent round robin discussions. Pose an issue or question and go once around the group, getting an answer from each participant. Give the right to "pass" for those who do not have an answer they wish to share.

Brainstorm lists of all kinds. Some examples. What are the pros and cons of this idea? How could we improve this? What else do we need to consider? What are all the problems we must anticipate? Who do we need to include? What are the risks and rewards? How could we use this information? And on and on… Make the list long, including everything. Then prioritize.

Get physical. Get people moving by asking that they change seats. Change groups. Write comments on flip chart pages. Draw pictures on flip chart pages. Stand up to present. Raise their hands to vote. Any physical movement keeps things lively. Submit questions via online means.

Complete the sentence. Pose a sentence starter and ask for participants to fill in the blank. For example, "When I think about this change I feel…" "When I picture myself one year from now, I see…" "One thing I think we must do to succeed is…"

Ask the group to set ground rules for meeting behavior. This is a group conduct contract. Write the list of ideas on a flip chart. Post the list. Evaluate meetings or training based on the list. Ground rule examples: no interrupting, turn off cell phones, don't blame, do solve problems, all should participate.

Toss the ball or any other object (rubber chicken, Frisbee, stress ball) to facilitate participation throughout the entire group. One participant holds the ball and shares. Next, he or she should toss the ball to a new participant who continues the discussion.

Ask for ideas for agenda items. Use the ideas to craft the agenda for the next meeting or training session.

Line them up. To speak, that is. Pose an issue or question. Then, ask that all who wish to speak, to raise their hands. Assign a speaking order for all those who raised hands.

Call on people. If someone looks like he/she has something to say but is a bit reluctant to speak up, check out your perception.

Like this. "Hank, you look as if you have something to say. Is that right?" Do this with sensitivity. Respect it if someone answers, "No, not right now please."

Use the clock. A minute or two before break or ending, say this. "We have just a minute left and I want to make sure everyone has had a chance to speak. Susan and Sarah, we have not heard from either of you. Any comments?"

Start with some fun. Ask that participants raise their right arms—straight up in the air. Then instruct that on the count of 3, participants should point at any person in the group. The person with the most fingers pointed at him or her should start the discussion.

Argue both sides of an issue or question. Divide the group into two teams. Assign each team a position. One team should be for an issue. One against. Participants do not need to agree with the assigned position to fulfill it. Ask each side to prepare arguments. Then hear those arguments in a sort of trial by jury fashion.

Pass it on. Ask each participant to write a question or problem on a piece of paper. Then, ask participants to pass their paper to the person on their right. That person should write an answer/comment/solution in response to the question or problem. After a minute, ask participants to pass the papers on person to the right one more time. Repeat the process of passing/writing as many times as you wish before papers are returned to the original author.

Play ball. Ask participants to write an answer to a question or issue on a sheet of paper, crumble the paper into a ball, and toss the ball somewhere across the room. Once the paper balls are tossed, participants should pick up a ball, smooth it out, and read the response aloud.

Seek First To Understand.

Stephen Covey said, *"Seek first to understand before seeking to be understood."*

This is especially good advice for a facilitator. If you want to give great answers, sound advice, solid direction, discover the needs of others first. Or, put more simply, listen before you speak. And...

Ask Great Questions! Questions accomplish many things. They get people involved. They get people thinking. Questions keep people's attention. They show interest and care. Questions can also bring to light vital information, opinions and answers.

Here's a list of powerful questions. You'll find at least one or two great questions to ask at meetings or in training.

What's your reaction to this step of the plan?

What ideas do you have to improve this?

What other ideas do you have to improve this?

How do you know that actually happened?

How do you know that's a problem?

What's the evidence to support what is being said?

What are the circumstances surrounding this?

Who was involved?

What happened?

What led up to this?

If you could have anything, what would you wish for?

What is your worst fear?

What is the best thing that could happen?

What is the worst thing that could happen?

What thought process led you to that conclusion?

What is the root cause?

How would you like to handle this?

How should we proceed?

What part do you play in the problem? Others?

How can management help? Hurt?

What are the barriers to progress?

How can we deal with the barriers?

What else could get in the way?

What resources do we need?

What is the next best step?

What is working in our favor?

How will we know we're on track?

How will we measure success?

How will this look when we're finished?

What are all the gains we can count on when this is accomplished?

What is the return on investment?

How much can we lose?

If we do lose, how will we recover?

What can we learn from the situation?

How will we communicate our needs, desires?

How can we sell others on the idea?

How can we keep management posted on progress?

How will we keep each other posted on progress?

How can we break the tie?

How can we move through this disagreement?

What are our commonalities?

What are the real differences?

What are the possible compromises?

What are all the possible options to consider?

How should we choose the best one?

What are the criteria for evaluating the options?

What are the priorities to consider?

What order should we do these in?

What have we left out?

How should we celebrate?

The questions really are more important than the answers. The questions get people thinking in ways that answers cannot. Questions open up possibilities; answers narrow possibilities. Questions stimulate problem solving and innovation; answers prepare for action. Questions expand the range; answers focus it. Questions invite accountability from many; answers keep accountability with answer-giver. And , during change, perhaps the most important benefit to questions is: questions get people thinking in ways that naturally overcome resistance. By contrast, answers—especially those that sound like dictates—can actually arouse resistance.

Yes, at times you'll want to give answers and, depending on your role in the organization, may be required to do so. Just make sure that you've asked the questions whenever and wherever possible, especially if getting others to learn is your goal. In addition, right along with asking questions, make sure you've listened carefully to what others have to say. There's no better way to get lots of minds working on your organization's changes.

A Model For Learning

Learning is much more than the acquisition of knowledge. Excellent learning results in behavior change. So, any significant organizational change relies on the "learning as behavior change" formula. People must be equipped to do much more than understand the change. They must be able to execute it.

Here is a sequence for designing a learning that results in more than merely the acquisition of knowledge, and prepares people to skillfully act. Use it for any learning opportunity to include: classroom, meetings, coaching, groups, one-on-one. The same sequence applies in all cases.

1. Tell Them Why

Why learn this information and acquire these skills? What's the value? How do the information and skills apply to work? What are the benefits to the individual, team, organization? Simon Sinek talks about the power of why in his now-famous TED Talk, during which he cites Apple as being excellent at talking "Why," before "What" and "How." Sinek believes talking "Why before What and How" is a key to Apple's success in the marketplace.

2. Tell Them What

What are the learning objectives? What will they be able to think, say, and do when the learning is done? Be specific. List categories of information and types of skills, chunking the bigger stuff into smaller pieces, so a larger task like 'make a peanut butter sandwich', for example, becomes a sequences of steps that can easily be learned.

3. Get Them Active

Adults like to actively participate in learning experiences. Lecture, while important to learning, ought to be delivered in limited doses and reinforced by other learning methods. Demonstrations. Discussion. Question and Answer. Assessments. Case Studies.

4. Check Progress

How effective is the learning? More specifically, how effectively can the learners execute the learning objectives when the training is done? Evaluate progress, both during learning and at the end of it. The best place to evaluate progress? On the job. Learning that's applied to the job is the best indicator of success.

5. Give Feedback

Tell them when they've got it right. Correct them when they've got it wrong. And, remember what Mary Kay said...

"Get ordinary people to do extraordinary things. Give them something simple and when they do it, praise the hell out of them."

YOUR NOTES:

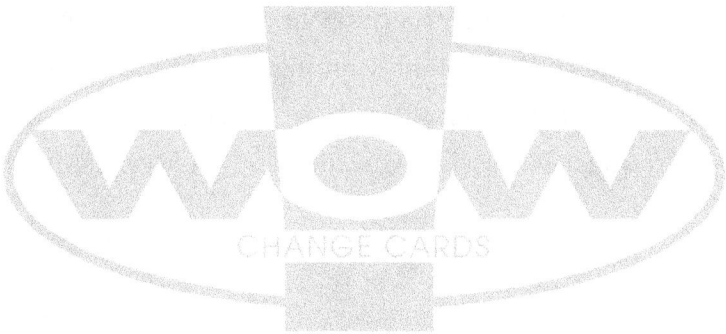

RECOMMENDED RESOURCES

The following list is only a small sample of the books we used in compiling the Wow! Change Cards. These are among our favorite resources for change.

John P. Kotter, *Leading Change*

Harvard Business Review, HBR's *10 Must Reads on Change Management*

Jeffrey Hiatt and Timothy Creasev, *Change Management: The People Side of Change*

Chip Heath and Dan Heath, *Switch: How to Change Things When Change Is Hard*

William Bridges and Susan Bridges, *Managing Transitions: Making the Most of Change*

Jeffrey Hiatt, *ADKAR: A Model for Change in Business, Government and our Community*

Jim Collins, *Good to Great: Why Some Companies Make the Leap...And Others Don't*

YOUR NOTES:

ABOUT CHRIS AND DEB

Christina M. Battell

Chris is the owner of Midwest Consulting Group, LLC providing coaching, training and consulting solutions to a variety of business and organizations. For the past 30+ years, Chris has developed and delivered solutions such as:

- Leadership Training and Coaching
- Conflict Resolution Training and Facilitation
- Management Development Training
- Team Building
- Performance Management Assessment
- Strategic Planning
- Event Facilitation

Email Chris: ChristinaMBattell@gmail.com

Deborah C. Miller, MA, MOQ/OE, PMP®

Deb is the owner of Miller Productivity, providing instructional design, project management, and procedural documentation services to financial services, healthcare, manufacturing and non-profit organizations. Deb is a Project Manager with 18+

years of experience leading projects and teams. She is a best-selling author and coach. Her services include:

- Instructional Design and Consulting for eLearning and blended courses.

- Procedure Analysis and Documentation

- Process Improvement

- Strategic Planning

- Change Management Assessments and Consulting

Email Deb at: DMiller@MillerProductivity.com

www.ingramcontent.com/pod-product-compliance
Lightning Source LLC
Chambersburg PA
CBHW070243200326
41518CB00010B/1666